IRISH TALES
of the Fairies and the Ghost World

Jeremiah Curtin

D0103845

DOVER PUBLICATIONS, INC.
Mineola, New York

Bibliographical Note

This Dover edition, first published in 2000, is an unabridged republication of a standard edition of the work first published in 1895 by David Nutt, London, under the title *Tales of the Fairies and of the Ghost World, Collected from Oral Tradition in South-West Munster.*

Library of Congress Cataloging-in-Publication Data

Curtin, Jeremiah, 1835–1906.
    [Tales of the fairies and of the ghost world]
    Irish tales of the fairies and the ghost world
       p. cm.
    Originally published: Tales of the fairies and of the ghost world.
London : D. Nutt, 1895.
    ISBN-13: 978-0-486-41139-2 (pbk.)
    ISBN-10: 0-486-41139-7 (pbk.)
    1. Tales—Ireland—Munster. 2. Ghosts—Ireland—Munster. 3.
Fairies—Ireland—Munster. I. Title.

GR153.6.M85 C87 2000
398.2'09419'01—dc21

                                  99-086376

Manufactured in the United States by LSC Communications
41139711   2018
www.doverpublications.com

Contents

Introduction	1
John Connors and the Fairies	5
Fitzgerald and Daniel O'Donohue	12
The Fairies of Rahonain and Elizabeth Shea	15
The Knights of Kerry—Rahonain Castle	19
The Cattle Jobber of Awnascawil	23
The Midwife of Listowel	27
Daniel Crowley and the Ghosts	30
Tom Daly and the Nut-Eating Ghost	34
Tom Connors and the Dead Girl	37
The Farmer of Tralee and the Fairy Cows	39
The Two Gamblers and the Fairies	42
The Girl and the Robber	46
Maurice Griffin and the Fairy Doctor	51
The Three Sisters and Their Husbands, Three Brothers	56
John Shea and the Treasure	64
St. Martin's Eve	70
James Murray and Saint Martin	74
Fairy Cows	76

John Reardon and the Sister Ghosts 79

Maggie Doyle and the Dead Man 83

Pat Doyle and the Ghost 85

The Ghost of Sneem 88

The Dead Mother 90

Tim Sheehy Sent Back to This World to Prove His Innocence 92

Tom Moore and the Seal Woman 94

The Four-Leafed Shamrock 96

John Cokeley and the Fairy 99

Tom Foley's Ghost 103

The Blood-Drawing Ghost 113

Murderous Ghosts 120

INTRODUCTION

Tales of the Fairies

D URING my travels in Ireland I made a stay of some time at the house of a farmer at a cross-road west of Dingle. Besides cultivating two farms, this man kept a small country store, near the famous Ventry Strand, had a contract to keep a road in repair, and was, in general, an active person. He had built an addition in two stories to his house, and the upper story he rented to me. The part which I occupied was at the intersection of the roads, and had windows looking out on both of them. Not far from the house was the chapel,* and about a mile beyond that the graveyard. The position was a good one from which to observe the people of the district as they passed to and fro on the two roads.

My host, Maurice Fitzgerald, was a man who knew the whole countryside well, spoke Gaelic with more ease than English, and held intimate relations with the oldest inhabitants. He knew the Gaelic name of every field within two miles of his house and the name of every hill, cliff, and mountain for many a mile. It may be stated here that in the Gaelic-speaking parts of Ireland there is a most complete system of naming every spot that needs to be distinguished from those around it. My host was a man who retained a belief in fairies, though he did not acknowledge it— at least, explicitly and in words.

"When I was a boy," said he, "nine men in ten believed in fairies, and said so; now only one man in ten will say that he

---

*In rural Ireland "chapel" means a Catholic church; "church," a Protestant church.

1

believes in them. If one of the nine believes, he will not tell you; he will keep his mind to himself."

It is very interesting indeed to find a society with even ten per cent. of the population professed believers in fairies. Of the remaining ninety per cent. a majority are believers without profession, timid believers, men without the courage of their convictions. The minority of the ninety per cent. falls into two parts, one composed of people of various degrees of belief in the fairy creed and philosophy, the other unbelievers. If one were to borrow the terms used in describing shades of difference in religious experience during our time, this minority might be divided into doubters, agnostics, and infidels.

The people of any purely Gaelic district in Ireland, where the language is spoken yet, preserve numerous remnants of pre-Christian belief, and these remnants are, in many cases, very valuable. Grotesque, naïve, and baseless they seem to observers almost always, but if the beliefs and opinions of the ordinary great ones of the earth be examined with due care, and with that freedom of spirit which is indispensable in such investigations, it will be found that many of them are not a whit more reasonable nor built on a better basis than the fairy creed of Ireland.

The people in Ireland have clung to their ancient beliefs with a vividness of faith which in our time is really phenomenal. Other nations have preserved large and (for science) precious heritages of superstition, but generally they have preserved them in a kind of mechanical way. The residuum of beliefs which they give us lack that connection with the present which is so striking in the case of the Irish. Certain divisions of the great Slavic race have preserved a splendid remnant of the old cosmic philosophy of pre-Christian times, and preserved parts of it with remarkable distinctness, but for all people who speak English the beliefs of the Irish contained in their tales have a near interest and a popular value that no similar productions of other nations are likely to attain.

As fairies are made to take such frequent part in Irish country life, and come to one's mind almost involuntarily when speaking of the supernatural in Ireland, I think it well to give in this connection some of the fairy tales and ghost stories told me at that house on the cross-road. These tales will show how vivid the belief of the people is yet, and will prove that fairies are not for all men personages of the past, but are as real for some persons as any other fact in life in this last decade of the nineteenth century.

After I had written down all the tales about Fin Mac Cool and other heroes that I could find in that region, I invited my host to come to me in the evening and bring two or three men to tell strange adventures of our own time, true tales of the district.

I was moved to this by what I had learned at the funeral of a man who had died from a fairy stroke a few days before, and by meeting two men who had been injured by similar strokes. One of the two was a farmer's son who had fallen asleep incautiously while near a fairy fort and was made a cripple for life; the other was a man of fairly good education, who, besides his English knowledge, read and wrote Gaelic. I was unable to obtain the details relating to his case, but the man who died had interfered with a fairy fort and hurt his hand in the act. The deceased was only thirty-three years old, a strong, healthy person, but after he had meddled with the fort his hand began to swell, and grew very painful. The best doctors were summoned, but gave no relief, and the man died from a fairy stroke, according to the statement of all, or nearly all, the people.

After supper the "man of the house" came with two other persons, and we passed a very interesting evening. One of the two visitors was a blind man named Dyeermud Duvane, about forty years of age, and born in the neighbourhood, who had been in America, where he lost his eyesight. He related to me somewhat of his life in the United States. He had been a worker in quarries, had been in charge of gangs of men in New England and the West. He had saved a considerable sum of money when he was placed over a gang of Italians in one of the quarries near Springfield, Mass. The Italians became enraged at him for some reason, and blew up the poor man in the quarry. He lost his sight, and lay in a Boston hospital till his money was gone. After that his friends sent him home, where he lives now in a very small way. Though blind, he found a wife, and with her lives in a little cottage, has a garden and a quarter of an acre of potatoes.

This blind man, though a sceptic by nature, knew some good cases of fairy action, and told the first story of the evening. The second man was seventy years old, white-haired, with a fair complexion, and blue eyes which were wonderfully clear and serious. This was a genuine believer in fairies and a rare example of one type of old Irishman. He lived near a fairy fort about a mile distant; his name was John Malone. His family and friends had suffered from fairies, and his daughter-in-law died from a fairy stroke.

After some preliminary conversation, the blind man began as follows:

John Connors and the Fairies

THERE was a man named John Connors, who lived near Killarney, and was the father of seven small children, all daughters and no sons. Connors fell into such rage and anger at having so many daughters, without any sons, that when the seventh daughter was born he would not come from the field to see the mother or the child.

When the time came for christening he wouldn't go for sponsors, and didn't care whether the wife lived or died. A couple of years after that a son was born to him, and some of the women ran to the field and told John Connors that he was the father of a fine boy. Connors was so delighted that he caught the spade he had with him and broke it on the ditch. He hurried home then and sent for bread and meat, with provisions of all kinds to supply the house.

"There are no people in the parish," said he to the wife, "fit to stand sponsors for this boy, and when night comes I'll ride over to the next parish and find sponsors there."

When night came he bridled and saddled his horse, mounted, and rode away toward the neighbouring parish to invite a friend and his wife to be godfather and godmother to his son. The village to which he was going was Beaufort, south of Killarney. There was a public-house on the road. Connors stepped in and treated the bystanders, delayed there a while, and then went his way. When he had gone a couple of miles he met a stranger riding on a white horse, a good-looking gentleman wearing red knee-breeches, swallow-tailed coat, and a Caroline hat [a tall hat].

The stranger saluted John Connors, and John returned the salute. The stranger asked where was he going at such an hour.

"I'm going," said Connors, "to Beaufort to find sponsors for my young son."

5

"Oh, you foolish man," said the stranger; "you left the road a mile behind you. Turn back and take the left hand."

John Connors turned back as directed, but never came to a cross-road. He was riding about half an hour when he met the same gentleman, who asked: "Are you the man I met a while ago going to Beaufort?"

"I am."

"Why, you fool, you passed the road a mile or more behind. Turn back and take the right hand road. What trouble is on you that you cannot see a road when you are passing it?"

Connors turned and rode on for an hour or so, but found no side road. The same stranger met him for the third time, and asked him the same question, and told him he must turn back. "But the night is so far gone," said he, "that you'd better not be waking people. My house is near by. Stay with me till morning. You can go for the sponsors to-morrow."

John Connors thanked the stranger and said he would go with him. The stranger took him to a fine castle then, and told him to dismount and come in.

"Your horse will be taken care of," said he, "I have servants enough."

John Connors rode a splendid white horse, and the like of him wasn't in the country round. The gentleman had a good supper brought to Connors. After supper he showed him a bed and said, "Take off your clothes and sleep soundly till morning."

When Connors was asleep the stranger took the clothes, formed a corpse just like John Connors, put the clothes on it, tied the body to the horse, and leading the beast outside, turned its head towards home. He kept John Connors asleep in bed for three weeks.

The horse went towards home and reached the village next morning. The people saw the horse with the dead body on its back, and all thought it was the body of John Connors. Everybody began to cry and lament for their neighbour. He was taken off the horse, stripped, washed, and laid out on the table. There was a great wake that night, everybody mourning and lamenting over him, for wasn't he a good man and the father of a large family? The priest was sent for to celebrate mass and attend the funeral, which he did. There was a large funeral.

Three weeks later John Connors was roused from his sleep by the gentleman, who came to him and said:

"It is high time for you to be waking. Your son is christened. The wife, thinking you would never come, had the child baptized, and the priest found sponsors. Your horse stole away from here and went home."

"Sure then I am not long sleeping?"

"Indeed, then, you are: it is three whole days and nights that you are in that bed."

John Connors sat up and looked around for his clothes, but if he did he could not see a stitch of them. "Where are my clothes?" asked he.

"I know nothing of your clothes, my man, and the sooner you go out o' this the better."

Poor John was astonished. "God help me, how am I to go home without my clothes? If I had a shirt itself, it wouldn't be so bad; but to go without a rag at all on me!"

"Don't be talking," said the man; "take a sheet and be off with yourself. I have no time to lose on the like of you."

John grew in dread of the man, and taking the sheet, went out. When well away from the place he turned to look at the castle and its owner, but if he did there was nothing before him but fields and ditches.

The time as it happened was Sunday morning, and Connors saw at some distance down the road people on their way to mass. He hurried to the fields for fear of being seen by somebody. He kept to the fields and walked close to the ditches till he reached the side of a hill, and went along by that, keeping well out of sight. As he was nearing his own village at the side of the mountain there happened to be three or four little boys looking for stray sheep. Seeing Connors, they knew him as the dead man buried three weeks before. They screamed and ran away home, some of them falling with fright. When they came to the village they cried that they had seen John Connors, and he with a sheet on him.

Now, it is the custom in Ireland when a person dies to sprinkle holy water on the clothes of the deceased and then give them to poor people or to friends for God's sake. It is thought that by giving the clothes in this way the former owner has them to use in the other world. The person who wears the clothes must wear them three times to mass one Sunday after another and sprinkle them each time with holy water. After that they may be worn as the person likes.

When the women of the village heard the story of the boys some of them went to the widow and said:

"'Tis your fault that your husband's ghost is roaming around in nakedness. You didn't give away his clothes."

"I did, indeed," said the wife. "I did my part, but it must be that the man I gave them to didn't wear them to mass, and that is why my poor husband is naked in the other world."

Now she went straight to the relative and neighbour who got the clothes. As she entered the man was sitting down to breakfast.

"Bad luck to you, you heathen!" said she. "I did not think you the man to leave my poor John naked in the other world. You neither went to mass in the clothes I gave you nor sprinkled holy water on them."

"I did, indeed. This is the third Sunday since John died, and I went to mass this morning for the third time. Sure I'd be a heathen to keep a relative naked in the other world. It wasn't your husband that the boys saw at all."

She went home then, satisfied that everything had been done as it should be.

An uncle of John Connors lived in the same village. He was a rich farmer and kept a servant girl and a servant boy. The turf bog was not far away, and all the turf at the house being burned, the servant girl was told to go down to the reek* and bring home a creel† of turf. She went to the reek and was filling her creel, when she happened to look towards the far end of the reek, and there she saw a man sticking his head out from behind the turf, and he with a sheet on him. She looked a second time and saw John Connors. The girl screamed, threw down the creel, and ran away, falling every few steps from terror. It was to the reek that Connors had gone, to wait there in hiding till dark. After that he could go to his own house without any one seeing him.

---

*A long pile of turf.   †Basket.

The servant girl fell senseless across the farmer's threshold, and when she recovered she said: "John Connors is below in the bog behind the reek of turf, and nothing but a sheet on him."

The farmer and the servant boy laughed at her and said: "This is the way with you always when there's work to do."

The boy started off to bring the turf himself, but as he was coming near the reek John Connors thrust his head out, and the boy ran home screeching worse than the girl. Nobody would go near the reek now, and the report went out that John Connors was below in the bog minding the turf. Early that evening John Connors' wife made her children go on their knees and offer up the rosary for the repose of their father's soul. After the rosary they went to bed in a room together, but were not long in it when there was a rap at the door. The poor woman asked who was outside. John Connors answered that it was himself.

"May the Almighty God and His blessed Mother give rest to your soul!" cried the wife, and the children crossed themselves and covered their heads with the bedclothes. They were in dread he'd come in through the keyhole; they knew a ghost could do that if it wished.

John went to the window of two panes of glass and was tapping at that. The poor woman looked out, and there she saw her husband's face. She began to pray again for the repose of his soul, but he called out:

"Bad luck to you, won't you open the door to me or throw out some clothes? I am perishing from cold."

This only convinced the woman more surely. John didn't like to break the door, and as it was strong, it wouldn't be easy for him to break it, so he left the house and went to his uncle's. When he came to the door all the family were on their knees repeating the rosary for the soul of John Connors. He knocked, and the servant girl rose up to see who was outside. She unbolted and unlatched the door, opened it a bit, but seeing Connors, she came near cutting his nose off, she shut it that quickly in his face. She bolted the door then and began to scream: "John Connors' ghost is haunting me! Not another day or night will I stay in the house if I live to see morning!"

All the family fastened themselves in a room and threw

themselves into bed, forgetting to undress or to finish their prayers. John Connors began to kick the door, but nobody would open it; then he tapped at the window and begged the uncle to let him in or put out some clothes to him, but the uncle and children were out of their wits with fear.

The doctor's house was the next one, and Connors thought to himself, "I might as well go to the doctor and tell all to him; tell him that the village is gone mad." So he made his way to the doctor's, but the servant boy there roared and screeched from terror when he saw him, ran to his master, and said, "John Connors' ghost is below at the door, and not a thing but a sheet on him."

"You were always a fool," said the doctor. "There is never a ghost in this world."

"God knows, then, the ghost of John Connors is at the door," said the boy.

To convince the boy, the master raised the upper window. He looked out and saw the ghost sure enough. Down went the window with a slap.

"Don't open the door!" cried the doctor. "He is below; there is some mystery in this."

Since the doctor wouldn't let him in any more than the others, John Connors was cursing and swearing terribly.

"God be good to us," said the doctor. "His soul must be damned, for if his soul was in purgatory it is not cursing and swearing he'd be, but praying. Surely, 'tis damned he is, and the Lord have mercy on the people of this village; but I won't stay another day in it; I'll move to the town to-morrow morning."

Now John left the doctor's house and went to the priest, thinking that he could make all clear to the priest, for everybody else had gone mad. He knocked at the priest's door and the housekeeper opened it. She screamed and ran away, but left the door open behind her. As she was running towards the stairs she fell, and the priest, hearing the fall, hurried out to see what the matter was.

"Oh, father," cried the housekeeper, "John Connors' ghost is below in the kitchen, and he with only a sheet on him!"

"Not true," said the priest. "There is never a person seen after parting with this world."

The words were barely out of his mouth when the ghost was there before him.

"In the name of God," said the priest, "are you dead or alive? You must be dead, for I said mass in your house, and you a corpse on the table, and I was at your funeral."

"How can you be foolish like the people of the village? I'm alive. Who would kill me?"

"God, who kills everybody, and but for your being dead, how was I to be asked to your funeral?"

"'Tis all a mistake," said John. "If it's dead I was it isn't here I'd be talking to you to-night."

"If you are alive, where are your clothes?"

"I don't know where they are or how they went from me, but I haven't them, sure enough."

"Go into the kitchen," said the priest. "I'll bring you clothes, and then you must tell me what happened to you."

When John had the clothes on he told the priest that, the day the child was born, he went to Beaufort for sponsors, and, being late, he met a gentleman, who sent him back and forth on the road and then took him to his house. "I went to bed," said John, "and slept till he waked me. My clothes were gone from me then, and I had nothing to wear but an old sheet. More than this I don't know: but everybody runs from me, and my wife won't let me into the house."

"Oh, then, it's Daniel O'Donohue, King of Lochlein, that played the trick on you," said the priest. "Why didn't you get sponsors at home in this parish for your son as you did for your daughters? For the remainder of your life show no partiality to son or daughter among your children. It would be a just punishment if more trouble came to you. You were not content with the will of God, though it is the duty of every man to take what God gives him. Three weeks ago your supposed body was buried and all thought you dead through your own pride and wilfulness."

"That is why my wife wouldn't let me in. Now, your Reverence, come with me and convince my wife, or she will not open the door."

The priest and John Connors went to the house and knocked,

but the answer they got was a prayer for the repose of John Connors' soul. The priest went to the window then and called out to open the door.

Mrs. Connors opened the door, and seeing her husband behind the priest she screamed and fell: a little girl that was with her at the door dropped speechless on the floor. When the woman recovered, the priest began to persuade her that her husband was living, but she wouldn't believe that he was alive till she took hold of his hand: then she felt of his face and hair and was convinced.

When the priest had explained everything he went away home.

No matter how large his family was in after years, John Connors never went from home to find sponsors.

Fitzgerald and Daniel O'Donohue

WHEN the blind man had finished, my host said: "There's many a story about that same Daniel O'Donohue, a fairy chief and King of Lochlein: Lochlein is the old name of the upper lake of Killarney. I used to hear many of those stories when I was young, but not one can I think of now. Sometimes the fairy chief was called O'Donohue of the Glen. There is a Knight of the Glen, too, near Killarney, and maybe he is the O'Donohue, for O'Donohue had a steed of the bells which the Black Thief was striving to steal, and so had the Knight of the Glen; but however that may be, I will tell you this:

"There was an old man named Fitzgerald, who lived in a neighbouring village. He was very fond of his garden, and spent all his time in it. One summer he had a beautiful field of 'white pink' potatoes. Once he had a fit of sickness, and was three days in bed. While the old man was keeping the bed the blight came on his potatoes and withered them.

"The saying was at that time that the fairies of Ulster were stronger than the fairies of Munster, and so they drove blight from Ulster to Munster.

"The fourth night the old man rose from his bed and crept out to take a look at his potato field, for his heart was in it. The night was very bright, the sky clear, and the moon full. He saw, sure enough, that the blight had come on his potatoes and destroyed them. He went into the house, took his blackthorn stick, and sat over the fire, and whittled it here and there. Then he went into the field with his bare head and feet, spat on his hand, took a firm grip on the stick, and, brandishing it, cried out time after time, as loud as he could, rushing the while from one end of the garden to the other: 'Daniel O'Donohue, come and take me with you to-night to the fairies and show me the man among them who destroyed my potatoes. I'll go with you to-night and to-morrow night and every night, if you'll bring me back to this spot again.'

"All the men and boys gathered around outside the ditch and listened to him, and he went on in this way a long while, calling on the chief fairy, Daniel O'Donohue, King of Lochlein, and challenging all the fairies of Ulster, and promising, if he couldn't do for them all himself, he had neighbours who would go with him and help him.

"At that time," said the host, "there wasn't a man in ten who didn't believe in the fairies and think that it was they who caused the blight, so they listened to the old man as he went on challenging the fairies of the North, offering his help to Daniel O'Donohue."

"The old man Fitzgerald was a strong believer in O'Donohue and the fairies," said I; "but have you ever known cases where fairies caused profit to one man and loss to another?" "I know just such a case," said he, "and here it is for you:

"About forty years ago there lived in this very town, and not half a mile from where we are sitting, a man named John Hanifin. He was a strong farmer, and had a large herd of cows; the cows were driven up every morning to the milking ground, a large open space in front of the house. In the centre of this space a large tub was placed, into which each servant girl poured her pail of milk as she filled it. One morning the tub was turned over and the milk spilled: the same thing happened the second morning and the third. No matter how they watched, or how careful they were, the milk was spilled always.

"Hanifin's wife was very angry, and scolded the girls so severely that they were in dread of her, and watched the tub more
closely each morning; but if they did, their watching was useless.
At the height of the milking the tub was turned over always and
the milk lost.

"One morning, when Hanifin was going to call the herder to
drive the cows to be milked he passed near an old fairy fort that
was on the road between the house and the pasture, and just as
he called to the herder he heard a child crying inside the fort: it
was crying for a drink, and the woman said: 'Be quiet a while;
Hanifin's cows are going home; we'll soon have milk in plenty.'

"Hanifin listened, but, like a wise man, said nothing. He went
home, and while the milking was going on himself watched the
tub and never let his eyes off it, and watched all that was going
on in the yard. This morning, as a maid was finishing the milking, a cow ran at a heifer that was walking across the yard near
the tub, pushed her against the tub, and overturned it. Out
came Hanifin's wife, scolding and blaming the girls. But Hanifin
stopped her, saying, ''Tis no fault of the girls; they can't help it;
I'll try and manage this.'

"He kept his mind to himself, said nothing to any one. The following morning he went as usual to call the herder to drive up the
cows, and, hearing the child crying in the fort, he, like the brave
man that he was, went inside the fort. He saw no one, but he said:
'A child is crying for milk. A cow of mine will calve to-morrow. I'll
let no one milk that cow: you can do what you like with her milk.'

"The tub was not turned over that morning, and never again
was it turned over. When the cow calved Hanifin's wife herself
was going to milk her, but Hanifin said, 'Leave her alone, I'll see
to that matter.' The woman insisted, and went out to milk. To
her amazement she found the cow milked and stripped already.

"The woman grew angry, thought that some of her neighbours were taking the milk from her; but Hanifin said he knew
all about it, and to leave the cow with him.

"Hanifin was going on well for two years, prospering in every
way, and he taking good care of the cow and never letting a girl
or a woman milk her. Whenever the wife tried to milk the cow
she found her stripped.

"Hanifin was a very soft-hearted man; some of his neighbours got into trouble, and he went security for them. At last, when they were not able to pay their debts, the creditors came on Hanifin, and there was an order against him for the whole amount.

"The bailiff came one day to drive off the cattle. Hanifin went to the fairy fort and said: 'I'm going to lose all my cattle, but I'll try to keep the cow I gave you and feed her still, so that the child may have milk.'

"Three bailiffs came and went down to the pasture across the field, but when they drove the cows up as far as the old fairy fort each bailiff was caught and thrown hither and over by people he couldn't see; one minute he was on one side of a ditch and the next minute on the other side. They were so roughly handled and bruised that they were hardly alive, and they not seeing who or what was doing it. The cattle, raising their tails, bawled and ran off to the pasture. The bailiffs, sore and wounded, went home and complained that people had abused and beaten them; 'that Hanifin, of course, put them up to it.' They were so cut and bruised that they had to give some account, and were ashamed to tell the truth.

"The following morning ten policemen and bailiffs went to take Hanifin's cattle, but when they were driving them up and got as far as the fort they were thrown head over heels, hither and over till they were terribly cut and beaten, and pitched into thorny bushes and holes till they were fools. The cattle, seeing this, took fright, bawled, raised their tails, and ran back to the pasture. The officers were barely able to leave the place. Never again did police or bailiff meddle with Hanifin's cows. The creditors never collected the money."

The Fairies of Rahonain
and Elizabeth Shea

WHEN the company came to my room on the following evening the host brought a fourth man, Maurice Lynch, a mason, who knew a good deal about ghosts and fairies.

When he bade me good-bye the night before, John Malone

promised to open the present session with a tale which he knew
to be true, for the chief actors in it were friends of his own, "and
himself was in it also." The tale was called forth by a question
concerning a practice among the fairies (quite common it
seems) of carrying away living people and leaving substitutes in
place of them. It seems that these substitutes are corpses when
the persons borne away are marriageable young women. When
a married woman is removed a deceased counterfeit is left to
take her place. When an infant is stolen a living imitation of the
child is put in the cradle. The substitute seems to the parents
their own child, but to any one who has the fairy vision the fraud
appears in its true form.

About thirty years ago, said the old man, there lived in a village near Rahonain Castle a man named James Kivane, a step-
brother of my own, and he married a woman called Elizabeth
Shea. Three or four nights after her second child was born
Kivane's wife, who was attended by her own mother and her
mother-in-law, woke and saw the bed on fire. She called to the
mother, who was there at the bedside, but had fallen asleep. The
mother sprang up, and, turning towards the hearth, saw a cat
with the face of a man on her, and was frightened, but she had
no time to look longer at the cat. When she had the fire
quenched she looked for the cat, but not a trace of her could they
find in the house, and they never caught a sight of her again.

Two days later the young child died, and three or four days
after that the woman had a terrible pain in her foot. It swelled to
a great size, and where the swelling was the skin looked like the
bark of a tree. The poor woman suffered terribly. They sent for
the priest many times, and spent money for masses. They offered
one priest twenty pounds to cure her, but he said that if all the
money in the kingdom were offered he would have nothing to do
with the case. He was afraid of getting a fairy stroke himself.

The foot was swelling always, and it was that size that a yard
of linen was needed to go once around it. The woman was a year
and a half in this way, and towards the end she said that horses
and carriages were moving around the house every night, but
she had no knowledge of why they were in it.

The mother went to an old woman, an herb doctor, and begged her to come and cure her daughter if she could.

"I can cure her," said the woman, "but if I do you must let some other one of your family go in place of her."

Now, as all the sons and daughters were married and had families of their own, the mother said she had no one she could put in place of this daughter. Kivane's wife used to raise herself by a rope which was put hanging above the bed. When tired and she could hold no longer, she would lie down again. The woman remained in suffering like this till a week before she died. She told her friends that it was no use to give her remedies or pay money for masses to benefit her; that it wasn't herself that was in it at all.

On the night that the mother saw the cat with a man's face and she sitting on the hearth, Kivane's real wife was taken by the fairies and put in Rahonain Castle to nurse a young child.

Nobody could tell who the sick woman was, but whoever she was she died, and the body was so swollen and drawn up that the coffin was like a great box, as broad as 'twas long. About a year after the funeral Pat Mahony, who worked for a hotel-keeper in Dingle, went to a fair at Listowel. At the fair a strange man came up to Mahony. "Where do you live?" asked the man.

"In Dingle," said Pat Mahony.

"Do you know families at Rahonain named Shea and Kivane?"

"I do," said Mahony. "Kivane's wife died about a twelvemonth ago."

"Well," said the strange man, "I have a message for you to the parents of that woman, Elizabeth Shea. She is coming to my house for the last nine months. She comes always after sunset. She lives in a fairy fort that is on my land. This is the way we discovered the woman: About nine months ago potatoes and milk were put out on the dresser for one of my servants who was away from home, and before the man came this woman was seen going to the dresser and eating the potatoes and drinking the milk. She came every evening after that for about a month before I had courage to speak to her. When I spoke she told me that her father, mother, husband, and child were living near Rahonain Castle. She gave every right token of who she was. 'I spent,' said she, 'three months in Rahonain, at first nursing a child that was in it, but was taken after that to the fort on the place where I am living now, in Lismore. I have not tasted food in the fort yet,' said she, 'but at the end of seven years I'll be forced to eat and drink unless somebody saves me; I cannot escape unassisted.'"

When Mahony came home to Dingle he went straight to Rahonain and told the woman's friends all that the strange man had told him. She had told the man, too, how her friends must come with four men and a horse and car; that she would meet them.

Mrs. Kivane's father and brother, and I and another neighbouring man, offered to go to Lismore, but Kivane wouldn't go, for he had a second wife at this time. The following morning we started, and went to the parish priest to take his advice. He told us not to go, and advised us in every way to stay at home. He was afraid, I suppose, that the woman might give the people too much knowledge of the other world. The other three men were stopped by the priest. Sure there was no use in my going alone, and I didn't.

Kivane's wife knew that her husband was married the second time, for she sent word to him that she didn't care, she would live with her father and her child. Everybody forgot the affair for a couple of years. When a retired policeman named Bat O'Connor was going from Lismore to Dingle, the woman appeared before him, saluted him, and asked was he going to Dingle, and he said he was. She told him then if he wanted to do her any good or service to go to her friends at Rahonain (she gave their names) and tell them that they had plenty of time yet to go and claim her; that she had not eaten fairy food so far. He promised to do as she asked. He reached Dingle soon after, went to Rahonain and told her friends what she had said. O'Connor, however, didn't tell everything in full till they would promise to go. At this the relations of Kivane's second wife went to O'Connor and bribed him to say nothing more. After that he was silent, and people cared no more about the woman.

The seven years passed, and at the end of that time Elizabeth Shea's father saw her one evening when he was coming home from market and was about a mile beyond Dingle. She walked nearly a mile with him, but didn't talk. At parting she gave him a blow on the face. On the following day he had to take to his bed, and was blind for seven or eight years. He kept the bed most of the time till he died. During the couple of days before he lost his sight Shea saw the daughter come in and give a blow to her child, which died strangely soon after. Neither priest nor doctor could tell what ailment was on the child.

About the time the child died Shea's second wife got sick, and has not milked a cow nor swept the house since. She has not gone to mass or market these twenty years. She keeps the bed now, and will keep it while she lives. She has no pain and is not suffering in any way, but is dead in herself, as it were. She had a fine young girl of a daughter, but she got a blow and died two days after. She has three sons, but Elizabeth Shea has never done them any harm.

The Knights of Kerry— Rahonain Castle

"Is there a story about the beginning of Rahonain Castle?" asked I.

"There is," said Maurice Fitzgerald, "and though I am not good at stories, I'll do the best I can and tell it to you."

Long ago, when the knights of Kerry were in Dingle and wished to build a castle in the neighbourhood, they went to a place above Ventry, and the chief knight set men to work there. When the men began work a voice came up through the earth, telling them to go home and not mind that place. They put their spades on their shoulders and walked away.

They went back to work on the following day, but if they did they heard the same voice telling them to leave that.

The men looked at one another, put their spades on their shoulders, and went back to Dingle.

On the third morning the chief knight put all the men to work in the same place, and stood watching them. The voice came through the earth and spoke to the knight, saying that if he wished to keep a fair name, to go away and leave the good people [fairies] in peace.

"Where am I to build my castle?" asked the knight.

"Beyond there at Rahonain," said the voice.

Work was begun at Rahonain, and as no place was provided for the workmen they went to people's houses in spite of them. If the man of a house wouldn't give what they wanted they would kill his cow or his pig, if he'd have the like, or they'd be vexing him in some way. If he had neither cow nor pig they'd give him a blow in the face, so the first other time he'd have something good for them.

Trant lived in Cahir a Trant at that time, and his nurse lived in Kil Vicadowny. The knight's men came across Trant's nurse, and the poor woman couldn't do well for them, for there was no one in the house but herself—she hadn't in the world but one cow and one pig. When the men were not getting what they wanted they killed the cow on the poor woman. As soon as she saw that she went over to Trant and told him her story.

"I can do nothing for you now," said he, "but the next other day they come send me word."

Some evenings after they came and she sent word. Trant came quickly. The men were inside, laughing and joking, making sport of the old woman.

"Were you not here a night before with my nurse?" asked Trant. "Why did you not conduct yourselves like men—take what she could give, and not kill her little cow?"

"We killed the cow," said one of them, "and 'tis the pig we'll take on her this turn."

Trant did nothing then but close the door and face the men. He took the ears off each one of them. He went out after that and took the tail and ears off each horse and let them all loose.

The men and the horses went home to the knight, who was raging when he saw them.

There was only a small chapel at Ventry, in the graveyard.

The knights were so proud they must enter the chapel before others. Common people had to wait outside till the knights went in, and when mass was over the people had to go first. The knights were the first to go in and the last to come out, and they stood always near the altar.

The Sunday after he cut the ears off the men, Trant went to mass on horseback and the wife behind him on a pillion. When he was riding along the strand and not far from the graveyard the horse stumbled and knocked himself and the wife.

"Come away home now," said the wife, "something will happen."

"I will not," said Trant, "and I don't care for the horse or what will happen."

After mass Trant was outside the chapel, the knights came out, caught him and killed him in the graveyard.

Trant's wife was at home; she turned back after the horse fell, but when she heard that her husband was dead in the church-yard she came to him, crying, and left her little son, nine months old, to another woman to nurse. While Trant's wife was keening over her husband the nurse hadn't patience to stay in the house, but ran out to the strand and left the child in a cradle alone. A banshee came then and took the child to a fairy fort half a mile beyond the church. When the nurse hurried back from the strand she found no sign of the child and was terrified. She searched through the whole house and around it, and as she didn't find the child anywhere she went running towards Kil Vicadowny to know did Trant's nurse take the little boy, but while she was going a voice called to her:

"Stop awhile and don't face that way: I'll tell you where the child is. It is not where you are going that he is, but in the fairy fort. If you do what I tell you and hurry you'll have him back; if not you'll lose him for ever. Run to that fort there beyond the graveyard, stop at the first house on the way, you'll find a skein of black flax thread inside in the house; put it around your left hand. You'll find a black-handled knife in the dresser, take that in your right hand and run; when you come to the fairy fort tie the end of the skein to a briar in the door of the fort; let the thread be unwinding from you till you are inside in the fairy kitchen. The child is there with a brown-haired woman, and she rocking him in a cradle. He has drunk twice of enchanted breast milk, and if he has the third drink you will never bring him home with you."

The nurse did all this, and did it quickly. She went into the house without saying a word. She caught the skein of flax thread and took the black-handled knife with her. She faced the fairy fort, tied the end of the skein to a briar, and let it unwind as she went till she came to the place where the woman was rocking the child in a cradle of gold. She raised the child and put the skein around him.

"A short life to the woman who gave you directions," said the brown-haired woman.

"I'll cross her," said the nurse, "and your curse will not fall on her."

When she was taking the child from the cradle the brown-haired woman gave him one blow on the cheek and said: "Take that and may it live long with you!" After that blow some of the Trants used always to go out of their minds. The child was brought home and grew up in good health. His grandfather was alive, but blind. When the boy was fifteen years of age the grandfather had three yearling stallions, and he told his men to put the best of the three in a stable for seven years and not to let him out for one moment.

At the end of seven years the grandfather sent for young Trant to come till he'd feel his bones to know were they hard enough.

"Mount the horse now," said the old man, when he had passed his hands over the grandson.

The horse was brought, and the young man mounted.

"Give him his head," said the grandfather, "but not too much of it when he's going towards the sea or the mountain."

Young Trant took his course back to Kil Vicadowny, and around the foot of Mount Eagle; from that he rode to Rahonain Mountain. He held on through high places, went far to the east, where he turned at last, and was making for home by the way of Ballymore.

One part of the cliff west of Ballymore goes farther toward the north than the rest of it. He was trying to turn the horse with the ridge, but he could not, so he gave him rein, and he jumped from the cliff, a distance of 220 feet, and the place is known as Trant's Leap to this day.

The grandfather had a watch out to know when the young man would be coming, and the stable doors were barred; he was in dread the horse would rush into the stable and kill the grandson. When the horse was home he ran to the stable, but the door to his own part was closed. He went from door to door then, but when all doors were closed he came back to his own place and stopped there.

The grandfather was led up, and put his hands on the young man to know in what way was he after the journey.

"Oh, you are able now," said he, "to knock satisfaction out of the knights for the death of your father. Come with me to the chapel next Sunday. When all the poor people go out I will stand in the door and you will work away inside on the knights with what strength there is in you."

When all the people were out on the following Sunday young Trant put his grandfather in the door and told him for God's sake to hold it. He went in and worked with his sword till he stretched sixty knights, all that were in it that day but one, who forced his way out between the legs of the old man and killed him.

Young Trant brought the grandfather home on his back, and that day was the last for the Knights of Dingle. The one knight who escaped through the door died of fright at the first place where he stopped, the place where the chief knight began to build the castle, and from that day the place is called Downall's Bed after him.

The Cattle Jobber of Awnascawil

"Do the fairies ever do harm for the pleasure of hurting people?" asked I of Maurice Fitzgerald.

"Whether they harm single men without reason I can't say," replied he, "but they injure a whole country-side sometimes."

"Oh, they do," said Duvane.

"I remember a story in which they punish a single man and destroy all the crops along the road they are travelling, and here it is for you."

There was a cattle jobber once who was going to a fair near Awnascawil, and he met the good people [fairies] about nightfall on the way. They took him with them and turned from the road into a lonely field in which was a large fairy fort. When they went in he saw a house as grand as any he had ever put foot in. The company ate and drank enough, and the good people pressed him to sit at the table, but he would taste neither food nor drink.

Next morning after breakfast they went out, leaving no one behind but their piper, whose name was Tim.

"You are not to let that man out of this while we are gone," said they to the piper.

The jobber noticed that when they were going, every one of the fairies dipped his finger in a box that hung by the door and rubbed his eyes. When the jobber thought that they were off a good distance he said to himself: "I'm man enough for this piper." With that he began to lace his shoes and prepare for his journey.

"What are you doing?" asked the piper.

"I'm going to be off out o' this," said the jobber. "I think it long enough that I'm here."

"You'll not leave this while I am in it," said the piper. "You heard the order to keep you here till they came back."

"Indeed then you'll not keep me, and I won't stay with you."

With that he rose, and no sooner was he on his feet than the piper caught him and they went at each other.

In the wrestling the jobber knocked Tim across a tub that was standing on the floor and broke his back. The piper didn't stir after that: how could he and his back broken. With that the jobber sprang to the door, put his finger in the box and rubbed one eye with the finger in the same way that he saw the fairies doing, and when his eye was rubbed he could see all the fairies in the world with that eye if they were before him, and not a one could he see with the other eye. He set forward then, spent one night on the road, and as the fair was to be held on the following day he stopped in a house not far from the fair ground. The day was close and warm and the jobber was thirsty, so he asked for a drink of water.

"You'll get it and welcome," said the woman of the house, "and it isn't water I'd give you to drink, but milk, if I could go for it, but I can't leave the cradle as something is the matter with the child since yesterday; neither I nor my husband slept a wink last night from taking care of him, and he screeching always."

"Well," said the jobber, "I'll take care of the cradle while you are after the milk, and sure the child will not die during that time."

The woman went for the milk, and the jobber rocked the cradle. He noticed that the screeching was different from the crying of a child, and caught hold of the blanket to take it from the child's face; but, if he did, the child had a firm grip of the clothes, and the jobber had to tear away the blanket. When he had the blanket away he saw what was in the cradle, and what was it, sure enough, but Tim the Piper. The man and his wife were young people, and the child was their firstborn.

"What brought you here, you scoundrel?" asked the jobber.

"Oh, when you broke my back," said Tim, "I could do nothing for the good people; they had no further use for me in the fort, so they put me here and took the child of the house with them."

"If you are here itself, why can't you hold your tongue and not be destroying the people with your screeching? Sure this is a good place you are in."

"Oh," said the piper, "I wouldn't cry, but for the rocking; it's the rocking that's killing me. It was you that broke my back, and don't expose me now."

"I'll expose you this minute," said the jobber, "unless you stop quiet."

"I'll stop quiet," said the piper.

When the woman came back the child was not crying. "What did you do to quiet him?" asked she.

"I only uncovered his face, and said that I'd kill him if he didn't stop quiet, and I suppose the child is in dread, as I am a stranger."

"You might as well stay the night with us," said the woman.

The jobber agreed, and as the child was quiet the mother could look to her work. When her husband came home in the evening she told him that the child had stopped crying since the stranger came, and the husband was glad.

"As the child is peaceable," said the jobber to the mother, "I'll take care of him to-night; you can go to bed."

The parents went to bed and left the child with their guest. About midnight the man saw that he was growing sleepy, and he pushed Tim and asked, "Couldn't you play a tune that would keep me awake?"

"It would be hard for me to play and my back broken," said

Tim, "but if I had the pipes and you'd prop me in the cradle I might play."

"Where are the pipes?"

"My pipes were brought here," said Tim; "they are on the corner of the loft above the fireplace."

The jobber rose up, took the pipes, and fitted them together. The piper began to play, and his music was so sweet that it could raise the dead out of the grave. He was not long playing when the father and mother heard the music, and they had never heard the like of it.

"Who is the piper?" asked the man.

"I am," said the jobber; "when I am on the road I play often to amuse myself."

Tim threw away the pipes then, stretched back, and stopped quiet till morning. The father and mother were glad that their child was resting. After breakfast the jobber asked the mother had they good turf, and she said they had. "Bring in two or three creels of it," said he.

She brought the turf, and he put it down on the fire. When the fire was blazing well the mother was outside. Said the jobber to Tim: "You were a bad host when I met you last, and you'll not be here any longer; I'll burn you now."

He went to the door then to call the mother. He wanted her to see what would happen, and not finding her he came back to the cradle, but found nothing in it except the clothes. Then he got terribly afraid that he would be brought to account for the child.

The mother came in and asked: "Where is my child?"

He told her everything. He and the woman went to the door to search for the piper, and what should the woman see outside the door but her own child. She was very glad then. The jobber gave her good-bye and started for the fair. On the way he felt a great storm of wind and hail coming towards him, and stooped down for shelter under a bush at the side of a ditch. When the storm was passing he saw that it was a legion of fairies destroying everything before them, tearing up potato stalks and all that stood in their way.

"Oh, shame!" cried the jobber, "to be ruining poor people's labour."

A slender, foxy, red-haired man, a fairy, turned towards him, and, putting his finger into the jobber's eye, took the sight from him. Never again did he see a fairy. When the foxy fairy went back to the [horde of fairies] he asked: "Did ye see that man who was with us in the fort, the man who broke the back of Tim the Piper, and did ye hear what he said?"

"We did not."

"Well, I saw him and heard him. I took the sight from him; he'll never see one of us again."

The jobber went to the fair, though he had but the one eye.

The Midwife of Listowel

"**W**HY do you call the fairies 'good people'?" asked I.

"I don't call them the good people myself," answered Duvane, "but that is what the man called them who told me the story. Some call them the good people to avoid vexing them. I think they are called the good people mostly by pious men and women, who say that they are some of the fallen angels."

"How is that?"

"They tell us that when the Lord cast down the rebel angels the chief of them all and the ringleaders went to the place of eternal punishment, but that the Lord stopped His hand while a great many were on the way. Wherever they were when He stopped His hand there they are to this day. Some of these angels are under the earth; others are on the earth, and still others in the air. People say that they are among us at all times, that they know everything that is going on, that they have great hope of being forgiven at the day of judgment by the Lord and restored to heaven, and that if they hadn't that hope they would destroy this world and all that's in it."

At this juncture the mason called out:

"I will not say whether I think the fairies are fallen angels or who they are, but I remember a case in which a woman lost an eye through the fairies."

"If you do," said I, "I hope you will tell it."

"I will indeed," said he.

There was an old woman, a midwife, who lived in a little house by herself between this and Listowel. One evening there was a knock at the door; she opened it, and what should she see but a man who said she was wanted, and to go with him quickly. He begged her to hurry. She made herself ready at once, the man waiting outside. When she was ready the man sprang on a fine, large horse, and put her up behind him. Away raced the horse then. They went a great distance in such a short time that it seemed to her only two or three miles. They came to a splendid large house and went in. The old woman found a beautiful lady inside. No other woman was to be seen. A child was born soon, and the man brought a vial of ointment, told the old woman to rub it on the child, but to have a great care and not touch her own self with it. She obeyed him and had no intention of touching herself, but on a sudden her left eye itched. She raised her hand, and rubbed the eye with one finger. Some of the ointment was on her finger, and that instant she saw great crowds of people around her, men and women. She knew that she was in a fort among fairies, and was frightened, but had courage enough not to show it, and finished her work. The man came to her then, and said:

"I will take you home now." He opened the door, went out, sprang to the saddle, and reached his hand to her, but her eye was opened now and she saw that in place of a horse it was an old plough beam that was before her. She was more in dread then than ever, but took her seat, and away went the plough beam as swiftly as the very best horse in the kingdom. The man left her down at her own door, and she saw no more of him. Some time after there was a great fair at Listowel. The old midwife went to the fair, and there were big crowds of people on every side of her. The old woman looked around for a while and what did she see but the man who had taken her away on a plough beam. He was hurrying around, going in and out among the people, and no one knowing he was in it but the old woman. At last the finest young girl at the fair screamed and fell in a faint—the fairy had thrust something into her side. A crowd gathered around the young girl. The old woman, who had seen all, made her way to the girl, examined her side, and drew a pin from it. The girl recovered.

A little later the fairy made his way to the old woman.

"Have you ever seen me before?" asked he.

"Oh, maybe I have," said she.

"Do you remember that I took you to a fort to attend a young woman?"

"I do."

"When you anointed the child did you touch any part of yourself with the ointment I gave you?"

"I did without knowing it; my eye itched and I rubbed it with my finger."

"Which eye?"

"The left."

The moment she said that he struck her left eye and took the sight from it. She went home blind of one eye, and was that way the rest of her life.

On the third evening the mason was absent, but his place was filled by a young farmer of the neighbourhood, named Garvey, who knew two ghost stories. The host was anxious that I should hear them, hence he brought in the farmer. After some hesitation and protests the young man told a story, which is grotesque enough and borders very closely, if it does not touch, on the unpermitted. It has some points of resemblance with the "Ghostly Concert" in "Tales of Three Centuries," which I translated from the Russian of Zagoskin. In Zagoskin's tale the demon leader of the ghostly orchestra in Moscow makes a guitar of the right leg of his victim, the only living man present at the midnight rehearsal. In this Irish tale the ghost makes an instrument out of his own body—plays on his ribs. There is a splendid tale among the Western Indians of North America describing a trial of skill in a musical contest between all existences in the universe except man. The first place was won by the lamprey eel (one of the forms of water as a person), and the eel was declared to be the greatest musician in the world. The lamprey eel in the contest uses his own body as a flute, played by inhaling air and then expelling it through his sides. Of those holes there are marks left on the body of the lamprey eel. Some Indians call water the Long One: and water is certainly a mighty musician.

Daniel Crowley and the Ghosts

THERE lived a man in Cork whose name was Daniel Crowley. He was a coffin-maker by trade, and had a deal of coffins laid by, so that his apprentice might sell them when himself was not at home.

A messenger came to Daniel Crowley's shop one day and told him that there was a man dead at the end of the town, and to send up a coffin for him, or to make one.

Daniel Crowley took down a coffin, put it on a donkey cart, drove to the wake house, went in and told the people of the house that the coffin was there for them. The corpse was laid out on a table in a room next to the kitchen. Five or six women were keeping watch around it; many people were in the kitchen. Daniel Crowley was asked to sit down and commence to shorten the night: that is, to tell stories, amuse himself and others. A tumbler of punch was brought, and he promised to do the best he could.

He began to tell stories and shorten the night. A second glass of punch was brought to him, and he went on telling tales. There was a man at the wake who sang a song: after him another was found, and then another. Then the people asked Daniel Crowley to sing, and he did. The song that he sang was of another nation. He sang about the good people, the fairies. The song pleased the company, they desired him to sing again, and he did not refuse.

Daniel Crowley pleased the company so much with his two songs that a woman who had three daughters wanted to make a match for one of them, and get Daniel Crowley as a husband for her. Crowley was a bachelor, well on in years, and had never thought of marrying.

The mother spoke of the match to a woman sitting next to her. The woman shook her head, but the mother said:

"If he takes one of my daughters I'll be glad, for he has money laid by. Do you go and speak to him, but say nothing of me at first."

The woman went to Daniel Crowley then, and told him that she had a fine, beautiful girl in view, and that now was his time to get a good wife; he'd never have such a chance again.

Crowley rose up in great anger. "There isn't a woman wearing clothes that I'd marry," said he. "There isn't a woman born that could bring me to make two halves of my loaf for her."

The mother was insulted now and forgot herself. She began to abuse Crowley.

"Bad luck to you, you hairy little scoundrel," said she, "you might be a grandfather to my child. You are not fit to clean the shoes on her feet. You have only dead people for company day and night; 'tis by them you make your living."

"Oh, then," said Daniel Crowley, "I'd prefer the dead to the living any day if all the living were like you. Besides, I have nothing against the dead. I am getting employment by them and not by the living, for 'tis the dead that want coffins."

"Bad luck to you, 'tis with the dead you ought to be and not with the living; 'twould be fitter for you to go out of this altogether and go to your dead people."

"I'd go if I knew how to go to them," said Crowley.

"Why not invite them to supper?" retorted the woman.

He rose up then, went out, and called:

"Men, women, children, soldiers, sailors, all people that I have ever made coffins for, I invite you to-night to my house, and I'll spend what is needed in giving a feast."

The people who were watching the dead man on the table saw him smile when he heard the invitation. They ran out of the room in a fright and out of the kitchen, and Daniel Crowley hurried away to his shop as fast as ever his donkey could carry him. On the way he came to a public-house and, going in, bought a pint bottle of whiskey, put it in his pocket, and drove on.

The workshop was locked and the shutters down when he left that evening, but when he came near he saw that all the windows were shining with light, and he was in dread that the building was burning or that robbers were in it. When right there Crowley slipped into a corner of the building opposite, to know could he see what was happening, and soon he saw crowds of men, women, and children walking toward his shop and going in, but none coming out. He was hiding some time when a man tapped him on the shoulder and asked, "Is it here you are, and we waiting for you? 'Tis a shame to treat company this way. Come now."

Crowley went with the man to the shop, and as he passed the threshold he saw a great gathering of people. Some were neighbours, people he had known in the past. All were dancing, singing, amusing themselves. He was not long looking on when a man came up to him and said:

"You seem not to know me, Daniel Crowley."

"I don't know you," said Crowley. "How could I?"

"You might then, and you ought to know me, for I am the first man you made a coffin for, and 'twas I gave you the first start in business."

Soon another came up, a lame man: "Do you know me, Daniel Crowley?"

"I do not."

"I am your cousin, and it isn't long since I died."

"Oh, now I know you well, for you are lame. In God's name," said Crowley to the cousin, "how am I to get these people out o' this. What time is it?"

"'Tis early yet, it's hardly eleven o'clock, man."

Crowley wondered that it was so early.

"Receive them kindly," said the cousin; "be good to them, make merriment as you can."

"I have no money with me to get food or drink for them; 'tis night now, and all places are closed," answered Crowley.

"Well, do the best you can," said the cousin.

The fun and dancing went on, and while Daniel Crowley was looking around, examining everything, he saw a woman in the far-off corner. She took no part in the amusement, but seemed very shy in herself.

"Why is that woman so shy—she seems to be afraid?" asked he of the cousin. "And why doesn't she dance and make merry like others?"

"Oh, 'tis not long since she died, and you gave the coffin, as she had no means of paying for it. She is in dread you'll ask her for the money, or let the company know that she didn't pay," said the cousin.

The best dancer they had was a piper by the name of John Reardon from the city of Cork. The fiddler was one John Healy.

Healy brought no fiddle with him, but he made one, and the way he made it was to take off what flesh he had on his body. He rubbed up and down on his own ribs, each rib having a different note, and he made the loveliest music that Daniel Crowley had ever heard. After that the whole company followed his example. All threw off what flesh they had on them and began to dance jigs and hornpipes in their bare bones. When by chance they struck against one another in dancing, you'd think it was Brandon Mountain that was striking Mount Eagle, with the noise that was in it.

Daniel Crowley plucked up all his courage to know, could he live through the night, but still he thought daylight would never come. There was one man, John Sullivan, that he noticed especially. This man had married twice in his life, and with him came the two women. Crowley saw him taking out the second wife to dance a breakdown, and the two danced so well that the company were delighted, and all the skeletons had their mouths open, laughing. He danced and knocked so much merriment out of them all that his first wife, who was at the end of the house, became jealous and very mad altogether. She ran down to where he was and told him she had a better right to dance with him than the second wife.

"That's not the truth for you," said the second wife; "I have a better right than you. When he married me you were a dead woman and he was free, and, besides, I'm a better dancer than what you are, and I will dance with him whether you like it or not."

"Hold your tongue!" screamed the first wife. "Sure, you couldn't come to this feast to-night at all but for the loan of another woman's shinbones."

Sullivan looked at his two wives, and asked the second one:

"Isn't it your own shinbones you have?"

"No, they are borrowed. I borrowed a neighbouring woman's shins from her, and 'tis those I have with me to-night."

"Who is the owner of the shinbones you have under you?" asked the husband.

"They belong to one Catherine Murray. She hadn't a very good name in life."

"But why didn't you come on your own feet?"

"Oh, I wasn't good myself in life, and I was put under a

penalty, and the penalty is that whenever there is a feast or a ball I cannot go to it unless I am able to borrow a pair of shins."

Sullivan was raging when he found that the shinbones he had been dancing with belonged to a third woman, and she not the best, and he gave a slap to the wife that sent her spinning into a corner.

The woman had relations among the skeletons present, and they were angry when they saw the man strike their friend. "We'll never let that go with him," said they. "We must knock satisfaction out of Sullivan!"

The woman's friends rose up, and, as there were no clubs or weapons, they pulled off their left arms and began to slash and strike with them in terrible fashion. There was an awful battle in one minute.

While this was going on Daniel Crowley was standing below at the end of the room, cold and hungry, not knowing but he'd be killed. As Sullivan was trying to dodge the blows sent against him he got as far as Daniel Crowley, and stepped on his toe without knowing it; Crowley got vexed and gave Sullivan a blow with his fist that drove the head from him, and sent it flying to the opposite corner.

When Sullivan saw his head flying off from the blow he ran, and, catching it, aimed a blow at Daniel Crowley with the head, and aimed so truly that he knocked him under the bench; then, having him at a disadvantage, Sullivan hurried to the bench and began to strangle him. He squeezed his throat and held him so firmly between the bench and the floor that the man lost his senses, and couldn't remember a thing more.

When Daniel Crowley came to himself in the morning his apprentice found him stretched under the bench with an empty bottle under his arm. He was bruised and pounded. His throat was sore where Sullivan had squeezed it; he didn't know how the company broke up, nor when his guests went away.

Tom Daly and the Nut-Eating Ghost

THE value of the next story (which was told by the blind man), apart from the comic in its form and contents, is the fact that nuts are buried for the godfather to eat after death. This is an interesting survival of primitive Gaelic belief.

Tom Daly lived between Kenmare and Sneem, but nearer to Kenmare, and had an only son, who was called Tom, after the father. When the son was eighteen years old Tom Daly died, leaving a widow and this son. The wife was paralysed two years before Tom's death, and could rise out of the bed only as she was taken out, but as the fire was near the bed she could push a piece of turf into it if the turf was left at hand.

Tom Daly while alive was in the employ of a gentleman living at Drummond Castle. Young Tom got the father's place, and he looked on his godfather as he would on his own father, for the father and godfather had been great friends always, and Tom's mother was as fond of the godfather as she was of her own husband. Four years after old Tom died the godfather followed him. He was very fond of chestnuts, and when he came to die he asked his friends to put a big wooden dish of them in his coffin, so he might come at the nuts in the next world.

They carried out the man's wishes. The godfather was buried, and the bed-ridden widow mourned for him as much as for her own husband. The young man continued to work for the gentleman at Drummond Castle, and in the winter it was often late in the evening before he could come home. There was a short cut from the gentleman's place through a grove and past the graveyard. Young Tom was going home one winter night; the moon was shining very brightly. While passing the graveyard he saw a man on a big tomb that was in it, and he cracking nuts. Young Daly saw that it was on his godfather's tomb the man was, and when he remembered the nuts that were buried with him he believed in one minute that it was the godfather who was before him. He was greatly in dread then, and ran off as fast as ever his legs could carry him. When he reached home he was out of breath and panting.

"What is on you," asked the mother, "and to be choking for breath?"

"Sure I saw my godfather sitting on the tomb and he eating the nuts that were buried with him."

"Bad luck to you," said the mother; "don't be belying the dead, for it is as great a sin to tell one lie on the dead as ten on the living."

"God knows," said Tom, "that I'd not belie my godfather, and 'tis he that is in it; and hadn't I enough time to know him before he died?"

"Do you say in truth, Tom, that 'tis your godfather?"

"As sure as you are my mother there before me 'tis my god-father that's in the graveyard cracking nuts."

"Bring me to him, for the mercy of God, till I ask him about your own father in the other world."

"I'll not do that," said Tom. "What a queer thing it would be to bring you to the dead."

"Isn't it better to go, Tom dear, and speak to him? Ask about your father, and know is he suffering in the other world. If he is we can relieve him with masses for his soul."

Tom agreed at last, and, as the mother was a cripple, all he could do was to put a sheet around her and take her on his back. He went then towards the graveyard.

There was a great thief living not far from Kenmare, and he came that night towards the estate of the gentleman where Tom was working. The gentleman had a couple of hundred fat sheep that were grazing. The thief made up his mind to have one of the sheep, and he sent an apprentice boy that he had to catch one, and said that he'd keep watch on the top of the tomb. As he had some nuts in his pockets, the thief began to crack them. The boy went for the sheep, but before he came back the thief saw Tom Daly, with his mother on his back. Thinking that it was his apprentice with the sheep, he called out, "Is she fat?"

Tom Daly, thinking it was the ghost asking about the mother, dropped her and said, "Begor, then, she is, and heavy!" Away with him, then, as fast as ever his two legs could carry him, leaving the mother behind. She, forgetting her husband and think-ing the ghost would kill and eat her, jumped up, ran home like a deer, and was there as soon as her son.

"God spare you, mother, how could you come!" cried Tom, "and be here as soon as myself?"

"Sure I moved like a blast of March wind," said the old woman; "'tis the luckiest ride I had in my life, for out of the fright the good Lord gave me my legs again."

Tom Connors and the Dead Girl

"THAT is a droll story, and may be true," said John Malone, "though it doesn't stand to reason that the mother could run as fast as her son, and he as much in dread of the man in the graveyard as herself. But, true or false, sure there is neither ghost nor fairy in it." "There is not," said Maurice Fitzgerald; "and now I'll give you, not a story, but an account of what happened to a man named Tom Connors, who lived beyond Dingle, and there's a ghost in it. Connors told me all himself, and it's only a year since he died."

In the year 1846 Tom Connors was working on the road between Slea Head and Ventry with other men. One morning he asked a fellow-workman for tobacco.

"I have only enough to last through the day," said the other, "but here are threepence for you, and at breakfast-time take your bread and walk up the road and you'll find an old woman selling tobacco. When you are paid next time give back the threepence to me."

"Very well," said Connors; and when it was breakfast-time he took his bread and went along the road, eating, till he came to where the old woman was, and bought the tobacco.

Before the next pay-day the man who loaned the threepence fell ill. Connors carried the money in his pocket a long time, hearing each day that the man was getting better, and expecting that he would see him the next day. One morning Connors was going to his work and had reached the bridge this side of Rahin. Just beyond that he saw the man who loaned him the money, and he coming toward him. The man was so near that Connors put his hand in his vest pocket and took out the threepence to pay him, but just then the man sprang on a ditch at right angles with the road and walked along on it over a bog.

Connors started to call to him, but stopped, watched, and saw the man jump from the ditch and cross a field; then he went behind a small mound, and that was the last of him. Connors walked on a short distance and met two men going to work. He saluted them, and asked what news had they. So and so died, said they, just before we left the house. This was the man who loaned Connors the threepence and had just crossed the bog. Connors said nothing to the two men about seeing him, at the time; but the eyes were leaving his head, he was in such amazement. Later, he gave the threepence to some poor persons and told them to pray for the man.

Fifty years ago it was a common thing to have dances wherever a fiddler happened to stop, and in those days strolling fiddlers were seen often. When Tom Connors, the man I mentioned, was young and unmarried, he found one evening that all the young people had gone away to dance; so he went on alone to Rahonain, for he thought it was there the dance was, but when he came to the place he was told that it was in the next village.

Connors started off towards the village without waiting. The place was lonely, and he had gone only a short distance past a forge by the wayside when he saw a woman following him. Thinking that she was some girl going to the dance, and that he could chat with her, he waited till she was near; he saw then that she was a girl who died some time before. He had danced with her often while she was in this world. He turned into a field to go by a short cut to the village; she followed. He said nothing, but hurried as much as he could; she was always close behind. Without saying a word, she was waiting for Connors to speak to her. When he reached the house where the dance was, young men and women were standing outside. The dead girl was right there behind him; he was terribly frightened, pressed in between the people and the house, and stood with his back to the wall. She went around and passed between the people and Connors—passed so near him that her clothes brushed his breast and her eyes looked into his eyes. Still he didn't speak to her. Then she went away across the field and disappeared.

The Farmer of Tralee
and the Fairy Cows

B EFORE any comment was made on Connors' experience of ghosts, Maurice Lynch, the mason, came in. My host asked him at once to tell a story, and the following is his contribution:

There was a rich farmer near Tralee, and he had a strong, able man of a son who was a herder for him, driving the cows and taking care of them always.

One evening the son was driving the cows to the field where they were to stop for the night. There was a fairy fort in the field. When the young man was driving the cows in at the gate of this field the first cow stretched her head through the gate, bawled as if some cow were horning her, and ran away. A cow with three dogs after her wouldn't be wilder than this one. He tried till he was tired to drive the other cows, and couldn't drive one of them into the field. He went home then and said he couldn't get a cow through the gate.

The farmer had three servant boys; they were inside in the house after the day, and he told them to go and help, but not a cow could they drive in, and they were in amaze, without knowing what was on the cows, and why they wouldn't go into the field as every evening before that. The farmer's son was with the boys, and when the four were tired, he said:

"There must be something before them." He went inside then and looked about the place, and what did he see standing aside from the gate but a little old man. He cursed the old man, raised his hand with a stick in it, and swore that he'd have his life.

"Stop your hand," said the fairy, "and don't try the like of that."

"I'll not stop my hand," said the young man, "for you have my stock destroyed."

"Wait," said the fairy, "and I'll tell you the cause of this trouble. I am very badly off from the want of a wife and a housekeeper, and what I wished was that yourself would come here till I spoke to you. I have the woman made out these four or five days, and we were to go for her to-night, and I want you to go with us. We have strength enough of our own men, but we can never take her without help from this world. You'll not lose by assisting me. I'll be your friend ever and always for the future."

"Well," said the farmer, "I'll help you."

"That's all I want," said the fairy, "and I'll not trouble your cows from this out. Be at the fort in half an hour and go with me."

The farmer's son was at the fairy fort at the time mentioned. The old man and a crowd of other fairies were waiting on horseback, and a horse was reserved for the young man. They started off and never stopped nor drew bridle till they reached the North of Ireland and halted at the house of a rich man, who had a very beautiful daughter. The fairies had struck her four or five days before; she was stretched on the bed and was to die that same night. She was given up by the priest and the fairies brought one of their own to put in place of her.

"You have no cause to be in dread of anything," said the old man to the farmer's son. "The house is full of our friends and neighbours; all you need to do is to take her with you out of the house and put her before you on the horse."

He did this, and soon they were back at the fort, and the old man said, "Put the lady off the horse and give her to me."

The farmer's son was grieved to think that such a fine young woman would be for ever with such an old fairy, and he said, "I'll not let her go with you; I want her myself."

He kept the woman from the fairy, and brought her with him to his father's house.

The old fairy began then at the father, who had more than forty cows and property of all kinds, and never stopped till he left him nothing but the walls of his house, and made beggars of the family. The young man and his wife were as poor as they could be, and one day the woman said to her husband, "If my father and mother knew our trouble we wouldn't be long the way we are, in poverty and want, and I'm sure it's the fairy that's working on us always."

"I'd wish to see them," said the husband, "and if I knew the place they are living in I'd try could I find them. Write a letter; I'll take it to them."

She wrote and mentioned many things that only she and her family knew. The husband started off; he had the name of the place, and was travelling always till he came to the right house at last. A fine house it was. There were herds of cows, and servants to milk them. The mother was down in her room when he came, and he saw her at once. The woman was crying. He asked her the cause.

"It seems," said she, "that you are a stranger in these parts."

"I am," said he.

"My only daughter is dead," said the woman, "and I am still grieving. Her father took to his bed after he buried her, and hasn't risen out of it since."

"Your daughter is alive yet; she didn't die at all."

"You'll suffer for that talk," said the mother.

He handed her the letter. She opened it and read. "That is her writing whether she is dead or alive," said the mother. She went to her husband then. "There is a man below in the room," said she, "who says that our daughter is living."

"Call him here to me. I'll put him in the way he won't say that again."

The wife showed the letter and said, "She wrote it; I know the hand."

They sent for the priest. "Don't harm the man," said the priest. "I'll write to the parish priest there and know the true story."

The parents had three sons besides the daughter they had lost, and these three brothers thought it long to wait. What they did was to saddle three horses and away with them, and never did they stop day or night, travelling and getting tidings. They kept in the right road till they made out the house. The sister put out her head when they were coming and knew her brothers. When she saw them she came very near fainting.

The sister told all about the fairy, and said, "Hurry away and bring my husband; don't leave it in the legs of the horses."

They turned, and never fear they didn't leave it in the horses, but took out of them what speed was in their bones. When they were within sight of their father's house they had handkerchiefs flying, they were so glad, and the people were running from every side to meet them. They made a great feast for the brother-in-law then, and asked him what stock had he lost by the fairy.

"Forty-five cows and two horses," said he.

The three brothers took sixty men with themselves and started for the fairy fort. The husband showed them where it was. They swore that if the old fairy were twenty fathoms deep they would have him out. They dug quickly, and not long were they working when they met a great flat stone. They were raising the stone with crowbars, when the fairy felt them. "Spare my house," cried he, "and I'll give help whenever ye need me."

"Give the man back all you took from him," said the brothers.

The fairy put back everything as it was before. The brothers left a blessing with their sister and her husband and went home. The fairy was a friend of the young couple after that. He never put the father nor the son back a pen'orth.

The Two Gamblers and the Fairies

A T our fourth meeting, which was held two nights later, the mason was present again, and told a story which had the same motive as the one which he had given us before, the stealing of a young woman made ill previously by a fairy stroke. The fairies leave a supposititious body, which is buried by the girl's parents, who mourn for their daughter, "and she living" in a distant part of the kingdom. There are endless variants on this theme; the earliest perhaps the more interesting.

There was a gambler once, and he went to a fair which was held near Killarney. He was at the fair a part of the day when another gambler came the way; the two began to play and held on till evening. When they finished at last there wasn't one penny gained by either of them on the other. The first gambler asked the stranger from what place was he, and he said, "I am from the North of Ireland." He asked him then would he join him for twelve months and they'd play in company. He consented. They agreed to make two halves of their gains, each to have one half.

The second gambler asked the first how much had he gathered, and he told him he had one keg full of gold. The first asked the second how much had he, and he said he had two kegs and the half of a third.

"Have you a family?" asked the second gambler.

"I have no one. Have you many with you?"

"I have no one but my mother."

"Then," said the first gambler, "we'll hire a horse and do you go for your gathering. We will live together. They hired a carman; the second gambler went with the carman and brought the three kegs. The carman was well paid when his work was done.

Not long after this it came in a dream to the first gambler that a keg of gold was dry on the strand. He called his comrade and said, "It came to me in a dream that there is a keg of gold high and dry on the strand." They rose up then, and taking two strong clubs went to the strand, searched every foot of it and met nothing. They were near the water as they were facing for home, when all at once they saw a great crowd. They didn't know who the people were, but it seemed like a large funeral.

"Go to them now," said the first gambler to the second, "and ask who they are and what brought them to this place so late at night."

"Indeed, then, I'll not go to them," said the second man. "I'll be off home for myself." And with that he left the first one alone.

The first man ran up with great speed till he came to the crowd, and what should he see but a coffin and four men carrying it. He gave a blow of his stick on the coffin lid, and asked, "What is here?" When he struck the blow and made the inquiry, the four men dropped the coffin, and the whole crowd vanished. In one twinkle of an eye there wasn't a man there—just as if the ground had swallowed them.

The man carried the coffin home on his back and took the lid from it. What did he find inside but the most beautiful young woman to be seen, and she asleep. He lifted her out of the coffin. She was alive, but tongue-tied—without a word. He said he'd give no quarter to the other man who deserted him and ran home. That night twelve months the first man dreamed again that if he would go to the strand he would find a keg of gold. "Rise up and come with me," said he to the second man.

"I saw enough the night I was with you last year. I'll stay where I am."

The first man went to the strand and searched, but if he did he found nothing. At last, as he was leaving the place, he saw a whole troop of fairies going towards a large fort, and he followed them. The fort seemed to his eyes in the night the grandest castle that ever was built. All the fairies sat down to supper, but he stood at the side of the door and looked at the nicest things in the world as they seemed to him. At last one of the fairies spoke up and asked, "Did ye see the man that carried the woman from us this time twelve months?"

"I did," said the chief, "and I know what he wants; he wants the young woman able to speak, and it will be a long time before he'll get that, though if she had three drinks out of this horn here she would speak in some way, but she will never speak rightly till the pin that I stuck in the top of her head is drawn from it. I put the pin there the night we carried her from her father and mother."

The horn was going the round of the fairies, and all were drinking from it. The gambler was watching his chance at the door. When he saw the horn near him he reached out his hand, snatched it, and raced away. No one followed him. He brought the horn home with him. The woman took three drinks from it and was partly cured; then he drew the pin. She gave a hearty laugh, and spoke as well as ever in her life.

The gambler was in dread of the fairies, so he took the horn to the fort and the fairies never troubled him.

The young woman, being cured now, wished her parents, who lived near Dublin, to know where she was.

"Write a letter," said the gambler. "I will take it, and be walking on till I come to them."

She wrote the letter. He took it and went away. He was inquiring always, and never stopped till he came to her father's house. All were in mourning, for she was a rich man's only daughter. Her father was lying on his bed when the gambler came, for he had never risen out of it since he buried the daughter. The fairies had put a strange body in place of her, and the father and mother thought that it was their own daughter they had buried.

"There is no business for you here," said the housekeeper.

"I have a letter to the master and mistress of this house from their daughter, and I will not go till I give it to them," said the man.

The housekeeper was going to bring servants to drive him out of the house, when the mistress came. She took the letter, read it, and went to her husband. "There is a man below in the kitchen," said she, "who says that our daughter is living, and that he has a letter from her."

The husband rose up in the bed. "Bring me the gun till I shoot that impostor!"

"Have patience," said the wife. "It's fitter for you to read the letter than to kill the man who brought it."

He read the letter, and, finding it true to all appearances, sprang out of bed, went to the young man, and questioned him. The man told the whole story.

The night that he saved her from the fairies was the same that the young woman died.

"Go home now," said the father, offering him money for the road. "I'll give you my daughter to marry if you bring her here to me."

"I have money enough of my own; I don't need yours," said the gambler, who was in dread the father might not keep his promise if he had the daughter at home. "Come with me and have the marriage at my place."

The father took a coach and four; himself, his wife, and the gambler rode away to find the daughter. The daughter wasn't in the house when they came, and the young man was in dread of his life; he thought the father would kill him if the daughter couldn't be found. She was on the brink of the sea, combing her hair, at the time. He found her at last, and when the parents saw their daughter they were near fainting.

After finding the daughter they thought the man too small, not good enough. He took them then to an inside room and showed his riches; he had a keg and a half, and the other gambler two kegs and a half full of gold.

"Have you as much as that?" asked he of the father.

"I have not," said he, "nor the third part of it."

Still he did not give him the daughter, but started for home, taking her with him. When they had gone some distance the mother said, "It is not right to act this way towards the man who saved our daughter from the fairies."

"He is the right man to be my husband," said the daughter. "I'd be among the fairies for ever but for him."

"Turn back and go to him," said the father. He left the daughter and she went back.

The gamblers divided their gold, and the second gambler went home, carrying his part to the north of Ireland.

The Girl and the Robber

THE next story, which was told by the blind man, contains an account of one important survival of old times: offering a beast to St. Martin. The method of curing a sick beast is also interesting.

The most solemn acts of worship in primitive times were connected with food and drink. Eating and drinking were, in fact, the main elements in public worship and thanksgiving. The moral of the story is that the young woman came to all her good fortune through her earnest endeavour to bring the sheep as an offering to St. Martin. When the story was finished the old man summed up the whole matter by remarking, "It was St. Martin did it all."

There was a farmer in the county Kerry who had a deal of cattle and sheep. He was a very rich man. There were four fairs in the year near his land, and one of these was held on St. Martin's day, Nov. 9. On that day they used to kill a sheep, heifer, or something to offer St. Martin. That was a custom all over Ireland, and is observed yet. When any sickness or ailment came over an animal suddenly a piece was cut out of its ear and melted for the sake of God and St. Martin. If the beast recovered it was never sold, but killed at home.

The wife of the rich farmer died and left a son and daughter after her. The man did not marry a second time, and the son and daughter grew till they were on the edge of being married. The brother and sister went to the fair on St. Martin's day, and while they were gone the father never thought once of killing something for St. Martin, as he used to do, and his father and grandfather before him.

It was late in the evening when the son and daughter came from the fair, and it wasn't five minutes before they came when the father remembered that he hadn't killed anything to honour St. Martin.

"A thing has happened this day that never happened before to myself, my father, or my grandfather," said he to the son.

"What is that?" asked the son.

"I never thought of bringing any animal to kill in honour of St. Martin."

"That you may be happy," said the son, "what a misfortune!"

"Never mind," said the father. "We can mend it. I wish you would go now and bring a wether.° Go up to the yard on the hill and bring him down to me."

"I may not come back alive if I go," said the son, "and as you hadn't anything to do all day, 'tis yourself ought to think of St. Martin's and have the sheep ready."

The son wouldn't be said by the father and wouldn't go; then the daughter said to the brother, "I'll go with you for the sheep." The brother swore that he wouldn't go alone nor in company. As he wouldn't go, the sister thought to herself, "I'll go without him." So she took a rope to tie the sheep.

In the parlour was a nice sword they used when in need of it; the sword was in a scabbard hanging from a belt. The young woman put the belt around her waist and went towards the hill. She knew very well where the sheep were. The place was a yard with a high stone wall around it which no dog or wolf could cross. Inside at one end was a little stone house where a herder could stay. She chose the best wether she could find, tied the rope on him, and started for home. Just as she was going a great fog fell, and she had no knowledge of where she was facing. She was going astray for a long time, and at last was very tired without making her way and sat down. "Well," said she to herself, "there is no use for me to be wandering and turning; I can never find the way home; I may as well stay where I am."

She was sitting a good part of the night in the field, when she

---

°A sheep castrated when very young, and raised for its tender meat.

thought, "I may as well let the wether go his own way and keep
the rope in my hand; he may take me back to the sheep; they'll
keep me company for the night." Before long the wether made
out the yard again. She sat down in the yard, and was just as if
at home with the sheep around her. "I'll make my way home
when the fog rises," thought she.

About midnight what should she hear but men talking, and
soon a good flock of sheep came into the yard and three men
behind them. Three brothers, such robbers that they troubled
the whole country, and there was a hundred pounds reward on
the head of each one of them. The robbers were coming from
the fair in disguise, and wanted to take something with them on
the way. The farmer was known through the country as a rich
man, and the robbers had walked the way before. When the girl
heard the men coming she hid in the stone hut at the end of the
yard and waited. One of the robbers was choosing the best
sheep, another was putting them with the new flock, and the
third man stood at the gate of the yard. The man taking the
sheep had a good many chosen when he saw the hut and said,
"Maybe 'tis here behind the best of the sheep are." He stooped
down and put in his head at the door. The girl had the naked
sword in her two hands. With one blow she took the head off the
robber and pulled him into the hut. The other two called and
asked what was keeping him. When no answer came the man
who was minding the sheep put his head into the hut; she served
him in the same way as the first one, took the head off him. The
third and youngest called to the others, but what use for him,
sure they couldn't answer. He went to the door, and what did he
find but his brother stretched. He pulled out the body and saw
that the head was gone from it. He made off with himself then
and left the two behind. The girl was afraid to come out, and
stayed where she was till clear day. She came out then and found
two flocks of sheep, for the robber had run away with his life.
She found the wether the rope was on and brought him home
with her. The father was crying and lamenting all night. He was
sure some evil had come to the daughter, so he welcomed her
with gladness and asked what kept her all night. She told him
how she had the two robbers killed and the yard full of sheep.

It's well pleased he was to see her safe. Himself and the son went then to the sheep yard, drew out the heads, and, taking the girl with them, went to where the reward was to be given. The girl received the two hundred pounds, which the father said must stay with her.

After that the report went all over the country that the young woman had done such a great deed of bravery, and all the people, young and old, were talking of her. About a year later, who should come the way to the farmer's house one evening but a man on horseback, and he dressed like any nobleman. His horse was put in the stable, where he got good food and care. After supper the farmer, who was wondering what could bring such a fine young man to his house, asked him,.who was he and what brought him?

"It is for a wife I came," said the young man.

"Oh, don't be talking," said the farmer, "my daughter is not a fit wife for the like of you."

"If she pleases me, isn't that enough?" asked the young man. "I have riches enough for myself; the two hundred pounds she got for the heads of the robbers is plenty for her. I want no fortune with her, I want nothing but herself."

Before the evening was over the farmer was full satisfied with the man, and the match was settled. The following morning they had the marriage and the wedding. The husband wouldn't stop another night, but said he must go home that very day. When the bride saw that he wouldn't stop she looked at him closely and thought to herself, "He may be a brother to the two men I killed." The young man mounted his horse and put the wife behind on a pillion. She had put the sword belt round her, and hid the sword under her long cloak.

The two rode away, and it was no fair road the man was travelling, but through lonely and wild places, and he never spoke a word till the middle of the afternoon when he stopped and said, "It's too long I'm waiting. I have the last of my patience lost, and I'll not give you more time. Come down from the horse."

"What are you saying?" asked she.

"You killed my two brothers in the sheep-yard," said the man. "I have you now, and I don't know in this world how will I make you suffer enough. It's not a sudden death, but a long punishment I'll give you." What did he tell her then but to undress till he'd strip the flesh bit by bit from her and she alive.

She came down from the horse. "Well," said she, "I've only one thing to ask."

"You'll get nothing from me," said the robber.

"All I wish is for you to turn your face from me while I'm undressing."

It was the will of God that he turned his face away, and that moment she gave one blow of her sword on his neck and swept the head off him. She hid the head among the rocks, where no dog or beast could come at it. There were two hundred pounds on the head of this man, for he was the worst of the brothers. She didn't know at first what to do, for she didn't know the road home. She sat on the horse and tried to turn him, but no step would he go for her. What did she do then but let the horse go his way, and he never stopped till he reached the robbers' house. There was no man in the house but a very old one, and when he heard the clatter he rose up and saw the horse. He saluted the farmer's daughter and asked where was his son.

"He is at his father-in-law's house," said she. "He got married this morning. He'll stop there to-night, and be here with the wife to-morrow. Friends will come with them to have a feast here; he sent me to tell you."

There was only one servant maid in the house, and the old man told her to make everything ready.

"This is a rich house," said the old man.

"Oh, how could your riches be compared with what your son's wife has?"

"I'll show you a part of this place," said the old man. He took her to a room, and gold and silver were there, not in a chest, but in heaps. "Look at this," said he.

"There is a deal of riches," said she, "but if there was as much more 'twould be less than the riches your son's wife has." Before supper she asked, was it far to a town or city?

"Cork is eight miles from this," said the old man, and he pointed out the road which led to the highway, a mile from the house. After supper the old man showed her a room and a bed. "You can sleep 'in this place' without fear," said he.

The room was full of men's clothes—coats, caps, and Caroline hats. She didn't sleep, but slipped off her own dress and put on a man's clothes. She started at midnight, took her dress with her, and travelled till daylight. She was within two miles of Cork then, and what did she see coming towards her but a young man on horseback. He saluted her, and said, "I suppose you are travelling all night."

"I am travelling a good part of it," said she, "and I suppose you are, as well as myself."

"Oh, I have to rise early. I am the Mayor of Cork, and have a deal of work on my hands," said he.

She threw herself on her knees when she heard this, and the Mayor asked what trouble was on her. She told of all that had happened. What he did was to tell her to stop there while himself would be going for men to the city. He went back and brought a good company of soldiers with two waggons, and they never stopped till they went to the robbers' house. The farmer's daughter went with the Mayor and some men to the place where she had the head covered. They brought the head with them, and gathered all the riches at the robbers' house, bound the old father, and took him to Cork, where the authorities hanged him. The Mayor was unmarried, and what did he do but marry the farmer's daughter and keep her as his wife while she lived.

Maurice Griffin and the Fairy Doctor

JOHN Malone had promised to give some information about doctors among the people, and tell how they got knowledge and power. When reminded of his promise, he told the following story:

There was a man at Dun Lean named Maurice Griffin. He was in service as a herder minding cows, and one morning while out with the cattle he saw something come down through the air in the form of a white cloud and drop on a hillock. It settled to be a lump of white foam, and a great heat rose out of it then.

One of the cows went to the hillock and licked the foam till she swallowed every bit of it.

When he went into breakfast Maurice told the man of the house about the cloud, and that it was a wonder to see the cow licking up what had settled on the hillock. "And it was white as any linen," said he.

When the man of the house sent the servant girl to milk the cow that evening he told her not to spill any drop of the milk till she had it brought to himself.

Maurice Griffin went with the girl, caught the cow, and held her. The vessel the girl was milking in did not hold half the milk. She did not like to leave the cow partly milked.

"Drink some of this," said she, "and let me finish, for it would spoil the cow to leave part of the milk with her."

Maurice Griffin emptied the vessel three times, drank all there was in it. The girl filled it the fourth time and went home with the milk. The master asked, "Was any of the milk spilled or used?" She told him truly, "This is the same vessel that I use always in milking, and that cow never filled it before till to-night. I didn't like to leave any milk with her, so I gave some to Maurice."

"It was his luck gave him all; 'twas promised to him, not to me," said the master. He was fonder of Maurice Griffin than ever, and Maurice began to foretell right away and cure people. The report went out through the country that all he foretold came to pass, and all he undertook to cure he cured. The priest, hearing this, didn't want to have the like of him in the parish, and spoke of him from the altar, but Griffin gave no answer. One morning the priest went to where Griffin was, saluted him, and was saluted in turn. "I hear that you are curing and foretelling," said the priest. "Where did you get the knowledge to foretell and to cure?"

"I foretell and I cure many persons, I serve people," said Griffin; "and my business is as good as yours. Some say that you have power, your reverence, but if you have, you are not fore-telling or curing."

"Well," said the priest, "I'll know can you foretell or not. Answer me a question, and if you can I'll believe you."

"I'll answer you any question you'll put to me," said Griffin.

"What time or minute of the day did the last new moon appear?"

"I will tell you that," said Griffin. "Do you remember that when you were passing Travug your horse stooped to drink and his right leg was first in the river? Under your neck you wear a stone which the Pope gave you; this stone always sweats three drops at the new moon; the stone sweated three drops when the horse's right foot touched the water, and that was the time of the new moon."

"Oh," said the priest, "what is rumoured of you is true; follow your hand, I'll not meddle with you from this out."

Griffin came home then and told the conversation. The master grew very fond of him after that, and having an only daughter he gave her to Maurice, and Griffin lived with his father-in-law till the old man died and left all he had to his son-in-law.

The people thought a deal of Maurice Griffin when he got the property, and they came for counsel and cure to him.

Griffin had two sons; in course of time he grew old and at last was very weak, and his first son, Dyeermud, managed the property. In those days everything was carried to Cork on horseback. Griffin called Dyeermud one day to him and said, "I am in dread that I am going to die. I don't want you to go to Cork to be absent so long."

"The company is going, and I'd like to go, too," said Dyeermud. "My brother is here: he will care for you and attend to everything while I am gone."

"I want you here," said the father, "for it's to you I will do all the good."

Dyeermud had a great wish to visit Cork.

"Go," said the father, "but you'll be the loser, and you'll remember my words."

Dyeermud went to Cork, and during his absence the father became very sick. Once, when the younger son was sitting at his bedside, the old man said, "I am in dread your brother will not be at home."

"What you were to leave him leave me," said the son.

"I cannot. I'll give you the gift of curing, but foretelling I could not give if I wished."

"How can you give the gift of curing?"

"I'll give it to you," said the father. "Go out to-night, kill a sheep and dress it, pick the right shoulder as clean as any bone could be cleaned from flesh, and in the night look over that bone, and the third time you look you'll see every one that you knew who is dead. Keep that bone with you always and sleep with it, and what you want to know to cure any disease will come to you from the bone. When a person is to be cured from a fairy stroke, look over the bone and a messenger will come from the fairies, and you will be able to cure those who come to you."

"As you will not give me the knowledge of foretelling, I will not take the curing. I will live honestly."

"I have no power to give you the knowledge," said the father, "but since you will not take the curing I will give it to your mother. The knowledge I can give to no one but your elder brother."

Griffin gave the curing to the wife. The knowledge he could give to no one but the elder son, and to him only if present.

Maurice Griffin died and was buried before Dyeermud came from Cork.

Dyeermud was astonished when he came and didn't find the father.

"You did badly not to stay," said the younger brother.

"Didn't I leave you?"

"You did, but he could leave the knowledge only to you."

"Why didn't he give you the curing?"

"He offered it to me, but I thought it too much trouble. I would use it if I had it. I let it go to our mother. She is old; let her have it. As he did not give me the knowledge I didn't want the curing. Maybe in after years when I have children it's on them the diseases I cured would come."

It was rumoured that the curing was with the mother, and the people were coming to her.

Once her godson got a fairy stroke in the leg, and she was vexed because his parents did not bring him quickly, for next day she would not be able to cure him at all. At last they came, and she was angry that they were so slow.

"You might have made bacon of him if you waited till morning," cried she. She cured him, and he was a very strong boy after that.

The parish priest had a sick horse left out to die. The clerk was very sorry, the horse was such a fine beast. "Wouldn't it be better to go to Mrs. Griffin?" asked he.

"Oh, how could she cure the horse?" asked the priest.

"I'll go to her," said the clerk.

"If you go to her," said the priest, "I give you no leave."

The clerk went, told Mrs. Griffin that he had come in spite of the priest, and to cure the horse if she could.

"It was the priest himself that injured the horse," said Mrs. Griffin. "He gave him water while hot from driving, and because the priest is fond of the horse he patted him and muttered something without saying God bless you. Go now, spit three times into the horse's ears, and say God bless you."

The clerk went and did this; the horse rose up as well and sound as ever, and the clerk brought him to the stable. The priest was astonished, and said, "They have a gift in the family: I'll not trouble them any turn again."

Mrs. Griffin was not able to give her gift to any one; the bone was buried with her.

When he had finished this story Malone said that there were different kinds of doctors, but that all received their power either through inheritance, "it was in the family," or by a sudden gift.

Herb doctors are in much esteem among country people, and gain their knowledge from supernatural sources. They don't learn: "it is given to them." The following are two cases cited by the old man.

In former times all the people had great faith in old women who were herb doctors. These women became doctors, not by learning different herbs, and studying, but by a supernatural power, and this power came to them always without their expecting it.

One woman of great name as a doctor got her power in this way. Three women were going to a village a mile out of Dingle. On the road they came to a small river, and there was no way to cross, but to walk through the water. All at once a fine lady stood before them, spoke very kindly to the first woman, and asked would she carry her over the river.

"Indeed, then, I will not: I've enough to do to carry myself."

The lady asked the second woman and received a like answer, but when the third woman was asked she said:

"I will carry you and welcome, and why not?" So she took the fine lady on her back, carried her over the water, and put her down on the dry bank.

The lady thanked her very kindly, and said, "When you wake to-morrow morning you will know all plants and herbs, you will know what their names are, and what virtues are in them."

Next morning when the woman woke she could call all plants and herbs by name, she knew where they grew, and knew the power of each, from that out she was a great doctor.

Another woman was at the seashore one day. After a time she turned to go home, and while on the way felt afraid, she began to tremble suddenly, and grow sick from dread. She felt that something unnatural was near her, looked behind, and right there saw some great dark form. The moment she looked it vanished, but from that out she knew all plants and herbs and was a very great doctor.

Sometimes the best doctors will leave off curing, for they say that curing will bring misfortune in the end to the doctors or their children. It is believed firmly that there is a compensation for all this supernatural knowledge, and for everything out of the usual course of things. All the people believe that priests have the power of curing if they would only use it, but they are unwilling to take on themselves the punishment for curing. In former days they took pity on poor people sometimes and risked their health to cure them.

The Three Sisters and Their Husbands, Three Brothers

AFTER an interval of two days we had our fifth and last meeting in the house at the cross-road. As the old man had told all his stories, and the blind quarryman had only one left, my host brought a tinker who had "walked the way" that day and was passing the night at the house. The tinker knew none of the old tales, but as the host said, "He has two stories that will knock a laugh out of the company, and they prove that women can outwit their husbands, as well as other men," we were curious to hear what he had to say, and he told the following:

In the county Cork, a mile and a half from Fermoy, there lived three brothers. The three lived in one house for some years and never thought of marrying. On a certain day they went to a fair in the town of Fermoy. There was a platform on the fair ground for dancing and a fiddler on the platform to give music to the dancers. Three sisters from the neighbourhood, handsome girls, lively and full of jokes, made over to the three brothers and asked would they dance. The youngest and middle brother wouldn't think of dancing, but the eldest said, "We mustn't refuse; it wouldn't be good manners."

The three brothers danced with the girls, and after the dance took them to a public-house for refreshments.

After a while the second brother spoke up and said, "Here are three sisters, good wives for three brothers; why shouldn't we marry? Let the eldest brother of us take the eldest sister; I will take the second; the youngest brother can have the youngest sister."

It was settled then and there that the three couples were satisfied if the girls' parents were. Next day the brothers went to the girls' parents and got their consent. In a week's time they were married.

Each of the three brothers had a good farm, and each went now to live on his own place. They lived well and happily for about ten years, when one market-day the eldest sister came to the second and asked her to go to Fermoy with her.

In those days women used to carry baskets made of willow twigs, in which they took eggs and butter to market. The second sister said she hadn't thought of going, but she would go, and they would ask the youngest sister for her company.

All three started off, each with a basket of eggs. After they had their eggs sold in the market they lingered about for some time looking at people, as is usual with farmers' wives. In the evening, when thinking of home, they dropped into a public-house to have a drop of drink before going. The public-house was full of people, chatting, talking, and drinking. The three sisters did not like to be seen at the bar, so they went to a room up stairs, and the eldest called for three pints of porter, which was brought without delay.

It is common for a farmer or his wife who has a ten-shilling piece or a pound, and does not wish to break it, to say, "I will pay the next time I come to town"; so the eldest sister said now. The second sister called for three pints, and then the third followed her example.

'Tis said that women are very noisy when they've taken a glass or two, but whether that is true or not, these three were noisy, and their talk was so loud that Lord Fermoy, who was above in a room finishing some business with the keeper of the public-house, could not hear a thing for their chat, so he sent the landlord to tell the women to leave the room. The landlord went, and finding that they had not paid their reckoning yet, told them it was time they were paying their reckoning and moving towards home.

One of the sisters looked up and said, "The man above° will pay all. He is good for the reckoning."

The man of the house, thinking that it was Lord Fermoy she was speaking of, was satisfied, and went up stairs.

"Have they gone?" asked Lord Fermoy.

"They have not, and they say that you will pay the reckoning."

"Why should I pay when I don't know them? We'll go down and see who they are and what they mean."

The two went down, and Lord Fermoy saw that they were tenants of his; he knew them quite well, for they lived near his own castle. He liked the sisters, they were so sharp-witted.

"I'll pay the reckoning, and do you bring each of these women a glass of punch," said he to the man of the house.

The punch was brought without delay.

"Here is a half sovereign for each of you," said Lord Fermoy. "Now go home, and meet me in this place a week from to-day. Whichever one of you during that time makes the biggest fool of her husband will get ten pounds in gold and ten years rent free."

"We'll do our best," said the sisters.

°"The man above" is God.

Each woman of them was anxious, of course, to do the best she could. They parted at the door of the public-house, each going her own way, and each thinking of what could be done to win the ten pounds and ten years' rent.

It had happened that the eldest sister's husband became very phthisicky and sickly a couple of years after his marriage and fell into a decline. On the way home the wife made up her mind what to do. She bought pipes, tobacco, candles, and other articles needed at a wake. She was in no hurry home, so 'twas late enough when she came to the house. When she looked in at the window she saw her husband sitting by the fire with his hand on his chin and the children asleep around him. A pot of potatoes, boiled and strained, was waiting for her.

She opened the door. The husband looked at her and asked, "Why are you so late?"

"Why are you off the table, and where are the sheets that were over you?" asked she as if in a fright; "or the shirt that I put on you? I left you laid out on the table."

"Sure I am not dead at all. I know very well when you started to go to the market, I wasn't dead then, and I didn't die since you left the house."

Then she began to abuse him, and said that all his friends were coming to the wake, and he had no right to be off the table tormenting and abusing herself and the children, and went on in such a way that at last he believed himself dead and asked her in God's name to give him a smoke and he would go up again on the table and never come down till he was carried from it.

She gave him the pipe, but didn't let him smoke long. Then she made him ready, put him on the table, and spread a sheet over him. Now two poles were stretched overhead above the body and sheets hung over and down on the sides, as is customary. She put beads between his two thumbs and a Prayer-book in his hands. "You are not to open your eyes," said she, "no matter what comes or happens." She unlocked the door then and raised a terrible wailing over the corpse. A woman living opposite heard the wailing, and said to her husband:

"Oh, it is Jack that is dead, and it is a shame for you not to go to him."

"I was with him this evening," said the husband, "and what could kill him since?"

The wife hurried over to Jack's house, found the corpse in it, and began to cry. Soon there was a crowd gathered, and all crying.

The second sister going past to her own home by a short cut, heard the keening and lamenting. "This is my sister's trick to get the £10 and ten years' rent," thought she, and began to wail also. When inside she pinched the dead man, and pulled at him to know would he stir; but it was no use, he never stirred.

The second sister went home then, and she was very late. Her husband was a strong, able-bodied man, and when she wasn't there to milk the cows he walked up and down the path watching for her, and he very angry. At last he milked the cows himself, drove them out, and then sat down in the house. When the wife came he jumped up and asked, "What kept you out till this hour? 'Twas fitter for you to be at home long ago than to be strolling about, and the Lord knows where you were."

"How could I be here, when I stopped at the wake where you ought to be?"

"What wake?"

"Your brother's wake. Jack is dead, poor man."

"What the devil was to kill Jack? Sure I saw him this evening, and he's not dead."

He wouldn't believe, and to convince him she said, "Come to the field and you'll see the lights, and maybe you'll hear the keening."

She took him over the ditch into the field, and seeing the lights he said, "Sure my poor brother is dead!" and began to cry.

"Didn't I tell you, you stump of a fool, that your brother was dead, and why don't you go to his wake and go in morning? A respectable person goes in mourning for a relative and gets credit for it ever after."

"What is mourning?" asked the husband.

"'Tis well I know," said she, "what mourning is, for didn't my mother teach me, and I will show you."

She brought him to the house and told him to throw off all his clothes and put on a pair of tight-fitting black knee breeches. He

did so; she took a wet brush then, and reaching it up in the
chimney, got plenty of soot and blacked him all over from head
to foot, and he naked except the black breeches. When she had
him well blackened she put a black stick in his hand. "Now," said
she, "go to the wake, and what you are doing will be a credit to
the family for seven generations."

He started off wailing and crying. Whenever a wake house is
full, benches and seats are put outside, men and women sit on
these benches till some of those inside go home, then those outside go in. It is common also for boys to go to wakes and get
pipes and tobacco, for every one gets a pipe, from a child of
three to old men and women. Some of the boys at Jack's wake,
after getting their pipes and tobacco, ran off to the field to
smoke, where their parents couldn't see them. Seeing the black
man coming, the boys dropped their pipes and ran back to the
wake house, screaming to the people who were sitting outside
that the devil was coming to carry the corpse with him. One of
the men who stood near was sharper-sighted than others, and
looking in the direction pointed out, said:

"Sure the devil is coming! And people thought that Jack was
a fine, decent man, but now it turns out that he was different.
I'll not be waiting here!" He took himself off as fast as his legs
could carry him, and others after him.

Soon the report went into the wake house, and the corpse
heard that the devil was coming to take him, but for all that he
hadn't courage to stir. A man put his head out of the house, and,
seeing the black man, screamed, "I declare to God that the
devil is coming!" With that he ran off, and his wife hurried after
him.

That moment everybody crowded so much to get out of the
house that they fell one over another, screeching and screaming.
The woman of the house ran away with the others. The dead
man was left alone. He opened one eye right away, and seeing
the last woman hurrying off he said:

"I declare to the Lord I'll not stay here and wait for the devil
to take me!" With that he sprang from the table, and wrapped
the sheet round his body, and away with him then as fast as ever
his legs could carry him.

His brother, the black man, saw him springing through the door, and, thinking it was Death that had lifted his brother and was running away with him to deprive the corpse of wake and Christian burial, he ran after him to save him. When the corpse screamed the black man screamed, and so they ran, and the people in terror fell into holes and ditches, trying to escape from Death and the devil.

The third sister was later than the other two in coming home from Fermoy. She knew her husband was a great sleeper, and she could do anything with him when he was drowsy. She looked into the house through a window that opened on hinges. She saw him sitting by the fire asleep; the children were sleeping near him. A pot of potatoes was standing by the fire. She knew that she could get in at the window if she took off some of her clothes. She did so and crawled in. The husband had long hair. She cut the hair off close to his head, threw it in the fire and burned it; then she went out through the window, and, taking a large stone, pounded on the door and roused her husband at last. He opened the door, began to scold her for being out so late, and blamed her greatly.

"'Tis a shame for you," said he. "The children are sleeping on the floor, and the potatoes boiled for the last five hours."

"Bad luck to you, you fool!" said the woman. "Who are you to be ordering me? Isn't it enough for my own husband to be doing that?"

"Are you out of your mind or drunk that you don't know me?" said the man. "Sure, I am your husband."

"Indeed you are not," said she.

"And why not?"

"Because you are not; you don't look like him. My husband has fine long, curly hair. Not so with you; you look like a shorn wether."

He put his hands to his head, and, finding no hair on it, cried out, "I declare to the Lord that I am your husband, but I must have lost my hair while shearing the sheep this evening. I'm your husband."

"Be off out of this!" screamed the woman. "When my husband comes he'll not leave you long in the house, if you are here before him."

In those days the people used bog pine for torches and lighting fires. The man, having a bundle of bog pine cut in pieces, took some fire and went towards the field, where he'd been shearing sheep. He went out to know could he find his hair and convince the wife. When he reached the right place he set fire to a couple of pine sticks, and they made a fine blaze. He went on his knees and was searching for the hair. He searched the four corners of the field, crawling hither and over, but if he did not a lock of hair could he find. He went next to the middle of the field, dropped on his knees, and began to crawl around to know could he find his hair. While doing this he heard a terrible noise of men, and they running towards him, puffing and panting. Who were they but the dead man and the devil? The dead man was losing his breath and was making for the first light before him. He was in such terror that he didn't see how near he was to the light, and tumbled over the man who was searching for his hair.

"Oh, God help me!" cried the corpse. "I'm done for now!"

Hearing his brother's voice, the black man, who was there, recognised him. The man looking for the hair rose up, and seeing his brothers, knew them; then each told the others everything, and they saw right away that the whole affair was planned by their wives.

The husbands went home well fooled, shame-faced, and angry. On the following day the women went to get the prize. When the whole story was told it was a great question who was to have the money. Lord Fermoy could not settle it himself, and called a council of the gentry to decide, but they could not decide who was the cleverest woman. What the council agreed on was this: To make up a purse of sixty pounds, and give twenty pounds and twenty years' rent to each of the three, if they all solved the problem that would be put to them. If two solved it they would get thirty pounds apiece and thirty years' rent; if only one, she would get the whole purse of sixty pounds and rent free for sixty years.

"This is the riddle," said the council to the sisters: "There are four rooms in a row here; this is the first one. We will put a pile of apples in the fourth room; there will be a man of us in the third, second, and first room. You are to go to the fourth room, take as many apples as you like, and when you come to the third room you are to give the man in it half of what apples you'll bring, and half an apple without cutting it. When you come to the second room you are to do the same with what apples you will have left. In the first room you will do the same as in the third and second. Now we will go to put the apples in the fourth room, and we'll give each of you one hour to work out the problem."

"It's the devil to give half an apple without cutting it," said the elder sister.

When the men had gone the youngest sister said, "I can do it and I can get the sixty pounds, but as we are three sisters I'll be liberal and divide with you. I'll go first, and let each come an hour after the other. Each will take fifteen apples, and when she comes to the man in the third room she will ask him how much is one-half of fifteen; he will say seven and a half. She will give him eight apples then and say: "This is half of what I have and half an apple uncut for you." With the seven apples she will go to the second room and ask the man there what is one-half of seven; he will say three and a half. She will give him four apples and say, "Here are three apples and a half and the half of an uncut apple for you." With three apples left she will go to the man in the first room and ask what is the half of three. He will answer, "One and a half." "Here are two apples for you," she will say then; "one apple and a half and the half of an uncut apple."

The eldest and second sister did as the youngest told them. Each received twenty pounds and twenty years' rent.

John Shea and the Treasure

YOU have two stories of wise women, said the blind man. Now I'll tell the story of a man who came to the knowledge of what gold was in the kingdom, and lost it all through his own foolishness:

Between Dingle and the village of Banog there lived one John

Shea, and he was a very poor man, though he worked late and early whenever he found work to do. At last he said that he'd be starving at home no longer, he'd go to some foreign country. So off he started one day and never stopped travelling till he came to Cork and found a ship bound for Lochlin, which the people call Denmark now.

Shea went on board the ship, and the captain asked where he was going.

"I don't care much where I go," answered Shea, "if I go out of this place."

"There is no use in your going to Lochlin," said the captain; "the people there kill every Irishman that comes to that country."

"It's all one to me," said Shea; "I might as well be killed by the Danes as die of hunger at home."

The captain raised anchor, sailed away with Shea on board, and reached Lochlin at last. John Shea stepped on shore and went along, not knowing or caring much where he went. While travelling he came to a cross-road and took the right hand. At one side of the road was a hedge neatly trimmed.

"This might lead to some house where I could find work," thought Shea. He travelled on and reached a fine mansion at last and went in to ask for employment. Inside he saw two old men bearded to the waist and one old hag bearded to the eyes.

"Where did you come from?" asked one of the old men.

"From Erin," said Shea.

"What brought you to Lochlin?"

"To tell you the truth, I was starving, and left home to find employment and food. I took shipping at Cork, and the captain I sailed with landed me here."

"Sit down," said one of the old men. "We will not eat you, never fear; and there is plenty of gold and silver to be had if there is any good in you. Come this way," continued the old man, rising.

Shea followed the old man, who led him to a small room. In the floor of the room was a flat stone, with a ring in the middle of it. "Lift this if you can," said the old man. Shea pulled, but thought if all the men in Erin were to try, they could not lift the stone.

"I cannot lift it now," said he; "but if I were in the country a while, and had more to eat, I think I could lift it."

The old man stooped down, both pulled, and together raised the stone.

Underneath was a barrel of gold. "I will give you some of this," said the old man. Shea filled his two pockets. When he had the gold, the two men talked as follows:

"What part of Erin did you come from?"

"From Banog, near Dingle."

"Are you well acquainted with Dingle?"

"Indeed then I am. And why shouldn't I be; don't I go there to mass every Sunday, and wasn't I reared in the neighbourhood?"

"Go home now, John Shea, and in Banog, two fields from your house, is a fairy fort, and a very fine fort it is. You have gold in plenty to take you home. When you are in Dingle go to the best meatshop in the town and buy a leg of mutton, then buy a load of turf—ten to twenty creels of it—build a good fire outside the fort and roast the leg of mutton. While the mutton is roasting, the smell of it will be over the place, the fort will open, and a cat will rise out of it and come towards you. Hide before the cat sees you, and from your hiding-place watch her. She will walk up to the mutton, eat all she can of it, then she will lie down near the fire and fall asleep. That is your time. When you have the cat killed the fort will open. Do you go in then. Inside you will find a basin, a towel, and a razor. Take these and bring them to me. Touch nothing else in the fort. If you do you may never come out of it."

When John Shea had these directions he came back to Erin and made his way to Banog, bought the mutton, and did everything according to the old man's wish. When the mutton was roasted the cat came out and ate all she wanted or was able to eat. She stretched out then near the fire and fell asleep.

John Shea stole up softly, caught the cat by the throat, strangled her, and threw her aside. Straightway a broad door in the fort was thrown open. John Shea walked in through the door. In the first room on his left he saw a basin, a towel, and a razor. He did not touch these, but walked on to the next room, and there he saw a barrel of gold. At sight of the gold he remembered the old man in Lochlin, and turned back at once.

He took the basin, the towel, and the razor, hurried away from Banog to Cork, and never stopped till he walked into the old man's mansion in Lochlin.

"Have you the razor, the basin, and the towel?" asked the old man.

"I have," said John Shea; "here they are."

The two old men and the hag were there as before; they hadn't changed one hair.

"Move up here now, John Shea," said the old man; "lather and shave me."

"Oh, then, I never was any good to shave," said John Shea, "but your head is not hard, and I'll do what I can on you."

He shaved the old man, and when he had him shaved it wasn't an old man at all that was in it, but a youth of nineteen. The next old man, seeing the brother so young, was dying to lose his own beard.

"You'll make a real barber of me," said Shea.

When the second old man was shaved he was eighteen years of age.

"For God's sake, shave me!" begged the hag.

"I never thought to shave a woman," said Shea; "but I can't refuse you."

Shea shaved the old hag, and she was a young girl of sixteen.

"Now," said the two brothers to John Shea, "since you have done so much good to us we'll take you hunting."

They went out hunting, and all the game they saw that day was one mouse. They brought the mouse home and boiled it. When John Shea had his part of the mouse eaten he knew where all the hidden gold was in Erin. Up he jumped from his seat.

"Musha, my God!" cried he. "I am the happiest man in the world this day. The devil a piece of gold is there in Erin but I know where it is. I'll be the rich man now!"

The two men, seeing John Shea jumping and hearing him screech from delight, said:

"There was never much power of keeping a secret in the Irish."

"He is not to be trusted," said the sister; "he would give away the secret. Let him have some of the mouse broth to drink."

The men gave him the broth. He drank of it and lost knowledge of all the treasures the moment he swallowed the broth. They gave him only money enough for his passage to Cork and told him to go his own way for himself, they had no further use for him.

John Shea went back to Banog, where he died in the famine year (1847), and was buried at public expense.

The preceding group of fairy tales are connected with the peninsula between the bays of Dingle and Tralee. The following tales were taken down west of the Killarney mountains, but between Dingle Bay and the Kenmare River, and relate to the southern half of Kerry.

In this mountainous region the Gaelic language is spoken generally by the older inhabitants, and in many places ancient ways of thinking are well preserved among people of fifty years and upward. Persons between thirty and fifty, though they know the old-time ideas, do not live in them altogether. As to people of the rising generation, their minds seem turned in another direction. They are not settled anywhere yet; some of them are seeking, others are drifting.

In general, the region is not one of rapid movement, and in many nooks and corners of it the past is well represented. The present tales touching fairies, ghosts, and various personages outside ordinary human life refer to actual beliefs. Some persons hold to these beliefs as firmly as possible; indeed, they are among the main articles of faith for a good number of the old people.

There are persons in the educated world who consider fairy tales as mere sources of amusement; there are others who look on them as too frivolous to be read by serious people. Both views are erroneous. Fairy tales contain the remnants of a religious system prior to Christianity. When these tales are collected and compared with each other and with that mass of Keltic literature extending from the twelfth to the present century, and which remains in manuscript in Dublin, London, Brussels, Rome, and elsewhere, we may expect to find a certain religious system, a certain philosophy of life and death, exhibited to us with a tolerable degree of distinctness.

In the fairy tales which I have collected so far, and in the conversation of the men who told them to me, I find a remarkable freedom of intercourse between the visible and the unseen worlds, between what we call the dead and the living—a certain intimate communion between what has been and what is. Unless in the case of old people, it can hardly be said that there is such a thing as death in the Keltic fairy philosophy. Children and young persons are removed; other bodies, apparently diseased or dying, are put in their places. The persons removed are taken to fairy mansions; if they eat they are lost to this life; if they refrain they have seven years in which return is possible.

This is only one item in the system of extra-human forces in Keltic belief. All that we find so far in Hero Tales or Fairy Tales in Ireland is in close connection with that pre-Christian religion which covered the earth and included all races of men, which, in its boundless variety, was essentially the same, whether we consider the Greeks and Hindoos or the Indians of North and South America. For this religion, raising the dead, travelling on the water, running through the air, are not exceptional or wonderful; they are of daily occurrence and common; they are not merely incidents in it, but part of its machinery. This old universal religion had many other ideas which acquired new associations after the Christian era and took on new names. It is most interesting to note how much of it survives yet, not only among the uninstructed but among the leaders of mankind.

I found two tales of St. Martin, which are given here. The first is curious as containing the man-eating ghost, which is common enough among the Slavs, but which I find now in Ireland for the first time.

The grey cows from the sea, in the second St. Martin story, seem of the same breed as Glas Gainach brought from Spain by Elin Gow and the Glas Gavlen stolen by Balor of Tory Island.

The sacredness of the plough chains is an interesting bit of agricultural lore in the story of John Reardon. The heated coulter of a plough is used in Ireland to force confession from a witch who prevents butter from appearing when milk is churned.

The ocular illusion by which one thing seems another, which causes Tom Connors to think that an old horse is his cow Cooby, is common among all peoples. I found some excellent illustrations of it in stories of the Modoc Indians of Oregon.

St. Martin's Eve
(told by John Sheehy)

IN Iveragh, not very far from the town of Cahirciveen, there
lived a farmer named James Shea with his wife and three children, two sons and a daughter. The man was peaceable, honest,
and very charitable to the poor, but his wife was hard-hearted,
never giving even a drink of milk to a needy person. Her
younger son was as bad in every way as herself, and whatever
the mother did he always agreed with her and was on her side.

This was before the roads and cars were in the Kerry
Mountains. The only way of travelling in those days, when a man
didn't walk, was to ride sitting on a straw saddle, and the only
way to take anything to market was on horseback in creels.

It happened, at any rate, that James Shea was going in the
beginning of November to Cork with two firkins of butter, and
what troubled him most was the fear that he'd not be home on
Saint Martin's night to do honour to the saint. For never had he
let that night pass without drawing blood in honour of the saint.
To make sure, he called the elder son and said, "If I am not at
the house on Saint Martin's night, kill the big sheep that is running with the cows."

Shea went away to Cork with the butter, but could not be home
in time. The elder son went out on Saint Martin's eve, when he saw
that his father was not coming, and drove the sheep into the house.

"What are you doing, you fool, with that sheep?" asked the
mother.

"Sure, I'm going to kill it. Didn't you hear my father tell me
that there was never a Saint Martin's night but he drew blood,
and do you want to have the house disgraced?"

At this the mother made sport of him and said: "Drive out the
sheep and I'll give you something else to kill by and by." So the
boy let the sheep out, thinking the mother would kill a goose.

He sat down and waited for the mother to give him whatever
she had to kill. It wasn't long till she came in, bringing a big tom-
cat they had, and the same cat was in the house nine or ten years.

"Here," said she, "you can kill this beast and draw its blood. We'll have it cooked when your father comes home."

The boy was very angry and spoke up to the mother: "Sure the house is disgraced for ever," said he, "and it will not be easy for you to satisfy my father when he comes."

He didn't kill the cat, you may be sure; and neither he nor his sister ate a bite of supper, and they were crying and fretting over the disgrace all the evening.

That very night the house caught fire and burned down, nothing was left but the four walls. The mother and younger son were burned to death, but the elder son and his sister escaped by some miracle. They went to a neighbour's house, and were there till the father came on the following evening. When he found the house destroyed and the wife and younger son dead he mourned and lamented. But when the other son told him what the mother did on Saint Martin's eve, he cried out:

"Ah, it was the wrath of God that fell on my house; if I had stopped at home till after Saint Martin's night, all would be safe and well with me now."

James Shea went to the priest on the following morning, and asked would it be good or lucky for him to rebuild the house.

"Indeed," said the priest, "there is no harm in putting a roof on the walls and repairing them if you will have mass celebrated in the house before you go to live in it. If you do that all will be well with you."

[Shea spoke to the priest because people are opposed to repairing or rebuilding a burnt house, and especially if any person has been burned in it.]

Well, James Shea put a roof on the house, repaired it, and had mass celebrated inside. That evening as Shea was sitting down to supper what should he see but his wife coming in the door to him. He thought she wasn't dead at all. "Ah, Mary," said he, "'tis not so bad as they told me. Sure, I thought it is dead you were. Oh, then you are welcome home; come and sit down here; the supper is just ready."

She didn't answer a word, but looked him straight in the face and walked on to the room at the other end of the house. He jumped up, thinking it's sick the woman was, and followed her to the room to help her. He shut the door after him. As he was not coming back for a long time the son thought at last that he'd go and ask the father why he wasn't eating his supper. When he went into the room he saw no sign of his mother, saw nothing in the place but two legs from the knees down. He screamed out for his sister and she came.

"Oh, merciful God!" screamed the sister.

"Those are my father's legs!" cried the brother, "and Mary, don't you know the stockings, sure you knitted them yourself, and don't I know the brogues very well?"

They called in the neighbours, and, to the terror of them all, they saw nothing but the two legs and feet of James Shea.

There was a wake over the remains that night, and the next day they buried the two legs. Some people advised the boy and girl never to sleep a night in the house, that their mother's soul was lost, and that was why she came and ate up the father, and she would eat themselves as well.

The two now started to walk the world, not caring much where they were going if only they escaped the mother. They stopped the first night at a farmer's house not far from Killarney. After supper a bed was made down for them by the fire, in the corner, and they lay there. About the middle of the night a great noise was heard outside, and the woman of the house called to her boy and servants to get up and go to the cow-house to know why the cows were striving to kill one another. Her own son rose first. When he and the two servant boys went out they saw the ghost of a woman, and she in chains. She made at them, and wasn't long killing the three.

Not seeing the boys come in, the farmer and his wife rose up, sprinkled holy water around the house, blessed themselves and went out, and there they saw the ghost in blue blazes and chains around her. In a coop outside by himself was a March cock.° He flew down from his perch and crowed twelve times. That moment the ghost disappeared.

Now the neighbours were roused, and the news flew around that the three boys were killed. The brother and sister didn't say

---

°A cock hatched in March from a cock and hen hatched in March.

a word to any one, but, rising up early, started on their journey, begging God's protection as they went. They never stopped nor stayed till they came to Rathmore, near Cork, and, going to a farmhouse, the boy asked for lodgings in God's name. .

"I will give you lodgings in His name," said the farmer's wife.

She brought warm water for the two to wash their hands and feet, for they were tired and dusty. After supper a bed was put down for them, and about the same hour as the night before there was a great noise outside.

"Rise up and go out," said the farmer's wife; "some of the cows must be untied."

"I'll not go out at this hour of the night, if they are untied itself," said the man. "I'll stay where I am, if they kill one another, for it isn't safe to go out till the cock crows; after cockcrow I'll go out."

"That's true for you," said the farmer's wife, "and, upon my word, before coming to bed, I forgot to sprinkle holy water in the room, and to bless myself."

So taking the bottle hanging near the bed, she sprinkled the water around the room and toward the threshold, and made the sign of the cross. The man didn't go out until cock-crow. The brother and sister went away early, and travelled all day. Coming evening they met a pleasant-looking man who stood before them in the road.

"You seem to be strangers," said he; "and where are you going?"

"We are strangers," said the boy, "and we don't know where to go."

"You need go no farther. I know you well, your home is in Iveragh. I am Saint Martin, sent from the Lord to protect you and your sister. You were going to draw the blood of a sheep in my honour, but your mother and brother made sport of you, and your mother wouldn't let you do what your father told you. You see what has come to them; they are lost for ever, both of them. Your father is saved in heaven, for he was a good man. Your mother will be here soon, and I'll put her in the way that she'll never trouble you again."

Taking a rod from his bosom and dipping it in a vial of holy water he drew a circle around the brother and sister. Soon they heard their mother coming, and then they saw her with chains on her, and the rattling was terrible, and flames were rising from her. She came to where they stood, and said: "Bad luck to you both for being the cause of my misery."

"God forbid that," said Saint Martin. "It isn't they are the cause, but yourself, for you were always bad. You would not honour me, and now you must suffer for it."

He pulled out a book and began to read, and after he read a few minutes he told her to depart and not be seen in Ireland again till the day of judgment. She rose in the air in flames of fire, and with such a noise that you'd think all the thunders of heaven were roaring and all the houses and walls in the kingdom were tumbling to the ground.

The brother and sister went on their knees and thanked Saint Martin. He blessed them and told them to rise, and taking a little table-cloth out of his bosom he said to the brother: "Take this cloth with you and keep it in secret. Let no one know that you have it. If you or your sister are in need go to your room, close the door behind you and bolt it. Spread out the cloth then, and plenty of everything to eat and drink will come to you. Keep the cloth with you always; it belongs to both of you. Now go home and live in the house that your father built, and let the priest come and celebrate Monday mass in it, and live the life that your father lived before you."

The two came home, and brother and sister lived a good life. They married, and when either was in need that one had the cloth to fall back on, and their grandchildren are living yet in Iveragh. And this is truth, every word of it, and it's often I heard my poor grandmother tell this story, the Almighty God rest her soul, and she was the woman that wouldn't tell a lie. She knew James Shea and his wife very well.

James Murray and Saint Martin
(told by Timothy Sheahy)

THERE was a small farmer named James Murray, who lived between this and Slieve Mish. He had the grass of seven cows, but though he had the land, he hadn't stock to put on it;

he had but the one cow. Being a poor man, he went to Cork with four firkins of butter for a neighbour. He never thought what day of the month it was until he had the butter sold in the city, and it was Saint Martin's eve at the time. Himself and his father before him and his grandfather had always killed something to honour Saint Martin, and when he was in Cork on Saint Martin's eve he felt heartsore and could not eat. He walked around and muttered to himself: "I wish to the Almighty God I was at home; my house will be disgraced for ever."

The words weren't out of his mouth when a fine-looking gentleman stood before him and asked: "What trouble is on you, good man?"

James Murray told the gentleman.

"Well, my poor man, you would like to be at home to-night?"

"Indeed, then, I would, and but for I forgot the day of the month, it isn't here I'd be now, poor as I am."

"Where do you live?"

"Near the foot of Slieve Mish, in Kerry."

"Bring out your horse and creels, and you will be at home."

"What is the use in talking? 'Tis too far for such a journey."

"Never mind; bring out your horse."

James Murray led out the horse, mounted, and rode away. He thought he wasn't two hours on the road when he was going in at his own door. Sure, his wife was astonished and didn't believe that he could be home from Cork in that time; it was only when he showed the money they paid him for the other man's butter that she believed.

"Well, this is Saint Martin's eve!"

"It is," said she. "What are we to do? I don't know, for we have nothing to kill."

Out went James and drove in the cow.

"What are you going to do?" asked the wife.

"To kill the cow in honour of Saint Martin."

"Indeed, then, you will not."

"I will, indeed," and he killed her. He skinned the cow and cooked some of her flesh, but the woman was down in the room at the other end of the house lamenting.

"Come up now and eat your supper," said the husband.

But she would not eat, and was only complaining and crying.

After supper the whole family went to bed. Murray rose at day-break next morning, went to the door, and saw seven grey cows, and they feeding in the field.

"Whose cows are those eating my grass?" cried he, and ran out to drive them away. Then he saw that they were not like other cattle in the district, and they were fat and bursting with milk.

"I'll have the milk at least, to pay for the grass they've eaten," said James Murray. So his wife milked the grey cows and he drove them back to the field. The cows were contented in themselves and didn't wish to go away. Next day he published the cows, but no one ever came to claim them.

"It was the Almighty God and Saint Martin who sent these cows," said he, and he kept them. In the summer all the cows had heifer calves, and every year for seven years they had heifer calves, and the calves were all grey, like the cows. James Murray got very rich, and his crops were the best in the county. He bought new land and had a deal of money put away; but it happened on the eighth year one of the cows had a bull calf. What did Murray do but kill the calf. That minute the seven old cows began to bellow and run away, and the calves bellowed and followed them, all ran and never stopped till they went into the sea and disappeared under the waves. They were never seen after that, but, as Murray used to give away a heifer calf sometimes during the seven years, there are cows of that breed around Slieve Mish and Dingle to this day, and every one is as good as two cows.

Fairy Cows
(told by William Keating)

IN the parish of Drummor lived a farmer, whose name was Tom Connors. He had a nice bit of land and four cows. He was a fine, strong, honest man, and had a wife and five children.

Connors had one cow which was better than the other three, and she went by the name of Cooby. She got that name because her two horns turned in toward her eyes. They used to feed her often at the house, and she was very gentle, and had a heifer calf every year for five or six years.

On one corner of Connors' farm there was a fairy fort, and the cow Cooby used to go into the fort, but Connors always drove her out, and told his wife and boys to keep her away from the fort, "for," said he, "it isn't much luck there is for any cow or calf that is fond of going into these fairy forts."

Soon they noticed that Cooby's milk was failing her and that she was beginning to pine away, and though she had the same food at home as before, nothing would do her but to go to the fort.

One morning when Connors went to drive his cows home to be milked he found Cooby in the field and her forelegs broken. He ran home that minute for a knife, killed and skinned the cow, made four parts of the carcase, put the pieces in a hamper, and carried the hamper home on his back.

What of the meat himself and family didn't eat fresh he salt-ed, and now and then of a Sunday evening or a holiday they had a meal of it with cabbage, and it lasted a long time.

One morning after Tom was gone to the bog to cut turf the wife went out to milk, and what should she see but a cow walk-ing into the fort, and she the living image of Cooby. Soon the cow came out, and with her a girl with a pail and spancel.

"Oh, then," said Mrs. Connors, "I'd swear that is Cooby, only that we are after eating the most of her. She has the white spots on her back and the horns growing into her eyes."

The girl milked the cow, and then cow and girl disappeared. Mrs. Connors meant to tell her husband that night about the cow, but she forgot it, they having no meat for supper.

The following day Tom went again to cut turf, the woman went to milk, and again she saw the cow go into the fort, and the girl come out with a pail and a spancel. The girl tied the cow's legs, and sitting under her began to milk.

"God knows 'tis the very cow, and sure why shouldn't I know Cooby with the three white spots and the bent horns," thought Mrs. Connors, and she watched the cow and girl till the milking was over and thought, "I'll tell Tom to-night, and he may do what he likes, but I'll have nothing to do with fort or fairies myself."

When Connors came home in the evening, the first words before him were: "Wisha then, Tom, I have the news for you to-night."

"And what news is it?" asked Tom.

"You remember Cooby?"

"Why shouldn't I remember Cooby, and we after eating the most of her?"

"Indeed then, Tom, I saw Cooby to-day, and she inside in the fort and a girl milking her."

"Don't be making a fool of yourself. Is it the cow we are eating that would be in thc fort giving milk?"

"Faith, then, I saw her and the three white spots on her back."

"But what is the use in telling me the like of that," said Tom, "when we haven't but two or three bits of her left inside in the tub?"

"If we haven't itself, I saw Cooby to-day."

"Well, I'll go in the morning, and if it's our Cooby that's in it I'll bring her home with me," said Tom, "if all the devils in the fort were before me."

"Ah, Tom, if it's to the fort you'll be going, don't forget to put holy water over you before you go."

Early in the morning Tom started across his land, and never stopped till he came to the fort, and there, sure enough, he saw the cow walking in through the gap to the fort, and he knew her that minute.

"'Tis my cow Cooby," said Connors, "and I'll have her. I'd like to see the man would keep her from me."

That minute the girl came out with her pail and spancel and was going up to Cooby.

"Stop where you are; don't milk that cow!" cried Connors, and springing toward the cow he caught her by the horn. "Let go the cow," said Tom; "this is my cow. It's a year that she's from me now. Go to your master and tell him to come out to me."

The girl went inside the fort and disappeared; but soon a fine-looking young man came and spoke to Connors. "What are you doing here, my man," asked he, "and why did you stop my servant from milking the cow?"

"She is my cow," said Tom, "and by that same token I'll keep her; and that's why I stopped the girl from milking her."

"How could she be your cow? Haven't I this cow a long time, and aren't you after eating your own cow?"

"I don't care what cow I'm after eating," said Tom. "I'll have this cow, for she is my Cooby."

They argued and argued. Tom declared that he'd take the cow

home. "And if you try to prevent me," said he to the man, "I'll tear the fort to pieces or take her with me."

"Indeed, then, you'll not tear the fort."

Tom got so vexed that he made at the man. The man ran and Tom after him into the fort. When Tom was inside he forgot all about fighting. He saw many people dancing and enjoying themselves, and he thought, "Why shouldn't I do the like myself?" With that he made up to a fine-looking girl, and, taking her out to dance, told the piper to strike up a hornpipe, and he did.

Tom danced till he was tired. He offered twopence to the piper, but not a penny would the piper take from him.

The young man came up and said, "Well, you are a brave man and courageous, and for the future we'll be good friends. You can take the cow."

"I will not take her; you may keep her and welcome, for you are all very good people."

"Well," said the young man, "the cow is yours, and it's why I took her because there were many children in the fort without nurses, but the children are reared now, and you may take the cow. I put an old stray horse in place of her and made him look like your own beast, and it's an old horse you're eating all the year. From this out you'll grow rich and have luck. We'll not trouble you, but help you."

Tom took the cow and drove her home. From that out Tom Connors' cows had two calves apiece and his mare had two foals and his sheep two lambs every year, and every acre of the land he had gave him as much crop in one year as another man got from an acre in seven. At last Connors was a very rich man; and why not, when the fairies were with him?

John Reardon and the Sister Ghosts

ONCE there was a farmer, a widower, Tom Reardon, who lived near Castlemain. He had an only son, a fine strong boy, who was almost a man, and the boy's name was John. This farmer married a second time, and the stepmother hated the boy and gave him neither rest nor peace. She was turning the father's mind against the son, till at last the farmer resolved to put the son in a place where a ghost was, and this ghost never let any man go without killing him.

One day the father sent the son to the forge with some chains belonging to a plough; he would have two horses ploughing next day.

The boy took the chains to the forge; and it was nearly evening when the father sent him, and the forge was four miles away.

The smith had much work and he hadn't the chains mended till close on to midnight. The smith had two sons, and they didn't wish to let John go, but he said he must go, for he had promised to be home and the father would kill him if he stayed away. They stood before him in the door, but he went in spite of them.

When two miles from the forge a ghost rose up before John, a woman; she attacked him and they fought for two hours, when he put the plough chain round her. She could do nothing then, because what belongs to a plough is blessed. He fastened the chain and dragged the ghost home with him, and told her to go to the bedroom and give the father and stepmother a rough handling, not to spare them.

The ghost beat them till the father cried for mercy, and said if he lived till morning he'd leave the place, and that the wife was the cause of putting John in the way to be killed.

John put food on the table and told the ghost to sit down and eat for herself, but she refused and said he must take her back to the very spot where he found her. John was willing to do that, and he went with her. She told him to come to that place on the following night, that there was a sister of hers, a ghost, a deal more determined and stronger than what herself was.

John told her that maybe the two of them would attack and kill him. She said that they would not, that she wanted his help against the sister, and that he would not be sorry for helping her. He told her he would come, and when he was leaving her she said not to forget the plough chains.

Next morning the father was going to leave the house, but the wife persuaded him to stay. "That ghost will never walk the way again," said she.

John went the following night, and the ghost was waiting before him on the spot where he fought with her. They walked on together two miles by a different road, and halted. They were talking in that place a while when the sister came and attacked

John Reardon, and they were fighting two hours and she was getting the better of the boy, when the first sister put the plough chains around her. He pulled her home with the chains, and the first sister walked along behind them. When John came to the house he opened the door, and when the father saw the two ghosts he said that if morning overtook him alive he'd leave the son everything, the farm and the house.

The son told the second ghost to go down and give a good turn to the stepmother; "let her have a few strong knocks," said he.

The second ghost barely left life in the stepmother. John had food on the table, but they would not take a bite, and the second sister said he must take her back to the very spot where he met her first. He said he would. She told him that he was the bravest man that ever stood before her, and that she would not threaten him again in the world, and told him to come the next night. He said he would not, for the two might attack and get the better of him. They promised they would not attack, but would help him, for it was to get the upper hand of the youngest and strongest of the sisters that they wanted him, and that he must bring the plough chains, for without them they could do nothing.

He agreed to go if they would give their word not to harm him. They said they would give the word and would help him the best they could.

The next day, when the father was going to leave the place, the wife would not let him. "Stay where you are," she said, "they'll never trouble us again."

John went the third night, and when he came the two sisters were before him, and they walked till they travelled four miles; then they told him to stop on the green grass at one side, and not to be on the road.

They weren't waiting long when the third sister came, and red lightning flashing from her mouth. She went at John, and with the first blow that she gave him put him on his knees. He rose with the help of the two sisters, and for three hours they fought, and the youngest sister was getting the better of the boy when the two others threw the chains around her. The boy dragged her away home with him then, and when the stepmother saw the three sisters coming herself and John's father were terrified and they died of fright, the two of them.

John put food on the table, and told the sisters to come and eat, but they refused, and the youngest told him that he must take her to the spot where he fought with her. All four went to that place, and at parting they promised never to harm him, and to put him in the way that he would never need to do a day's work, nor his children after him, if he had any. The eldest sister told him to come on the following night, and to bring a spade with him; she would tell him, she said, her whole history from first to last.

He went, and what she told him was this: Long ago her father was one of the richest men in all Ireland; her mother died when the three sisters were very young, and ten or twelve years after the father died, and left the care of all the wealth and treasures in the castle to herself, telling her to make three equal parts of it, and to let herself and each of the other two sisters have one of these parts. But she was in love with a young man unknown to her father, and one night when the two sisters were fast asleep, and she thought if she killed them she would have the whole fortune for herself and her husband, she took a knife and cut their throats, and when she had them killed she got sorry and did the same to herself. The sentence put on them was that none of the three was to have rest or peace till some man without fear would come and conquer them, and John was the first to attempt this.

She took him then to her father's castle—only the ruins of it were standing, no roof and only some of the walls, and showed where all the riches and treasures were. John, to make sure, took his spade and dug away, dug with what strength was in him, and just before daybreak he came to the treasure. That moment the three sisters left good health with him, turned into three doves, and flew away.

He had riches enough for himself and for seven generations after him.

One day an old woman leaning on a staff and a blind man "walked the way to me." After some talk and delay they agreed to tell what they knew about fairies, ghosts, and buried treasures. I had heard of them before, and tried to secure their services. The old woman speaks English only when forced to it, and then very badly. The blind man has suffered peculiarly from the fairies. They have lamed the poor fellow, taken his eyesight, and have barely left the life in him. I shall have occasion to refer to the man later on. The woman told me three stories; one of them was an incident in her own experience, the other two concerned her husband's relatives.

The first story has nothing supernatural in it, though some of the actors were convinced firmly for a time that it had.

I may say that the woman, whose name is Maggie Doyle, was unwilling to tell tales in the daytime. It was only after some persuasion and an extra reward that she was induced to begin, as follows:

Maggie Doyle and the Dead Man

LONG ago, when I was a fine, strong girl, not the like of what I am this day, I went down the country with a bag of seamoss to sell. I was in company with a girl from the next village, and she was carrying another bag. Coming evening, the other girl found lodgings for the night with a friend, and I walked ahead on the road for myself. I wasn't long walking when I met a woman, and she took me home with her. It was milking time when we came. The woman, whose name was Peggy Driscoll, put cream into a churn, and told me to churn while herself would be milking.

I churned away while she was with the cows, and when the milking was over, she helped me, and the two of us were churning till the butter came. She never asked me to take a bite or a sup, not even a drink of butter-milk. I had food of my own with me, and made a supper of that. After supper she said: "There is a dead man above in the room; come with me." "Oh, God save us!" said I, "how is that, and who is it?" "My own husband, John Driscoll, and he's dead these three hours."

"God knows, then," thought I to myself, "'tis easy enough you are taking his death."

She brought warm water, and we went up, the two of us; we prepared the body of John Driscoll, dressed it, and laid it out, and put beads in the hands of the dead man, who was stiff and cold.

"I must go out now for a little start," said Peggy Driscoll; "sure you'll not be in dread of the corpse while I go to tell some of the neighbours that John is dead."

I was that in dread that it failed me to speak to her. The next minute she was gone and the door closed behind her. I was left alone with the corpse. I stopped there a while and went then to the kitchen, sat there a quarter of an hour, and went back to the dead man.

About midnight the woman of the house walked in, and with her a neighbouring young farmer. She made tea in the kitchen, and the two were eating and drinking for themselves with great pleasure, laughing and joking. They were talking English. I hadn't but two or three words of English at that time, and John Driscoll not a word at all, but after a while the young farmer laughed, and, forgetting himself, said in Irish:

"It's a happy woman you are this night, Peggy, and the old man above on the table."

With that, the corpse sprang up, tumbling candles and everything before him. He caught a pike that was in the corner, and down to the kitchen with him. Peggy Driscoll and the young farmer began to screech in the way you'd think the life would leave the two of them, but by my word they hadn't long to screech in the kitchen, for the pike was coming at them. Out with the two through the back door and John Driscoll at their heels. I took my bag and away with me through the front door. I was running for hours and hurrying on. I didn't know where was I going, till at last I met a man, and asked what was the next town, and he said Killarney. I went on till I came to Killarney, and sold my bag of sea-moss to the first buyer, and took the road home for myself.

"Did you go to Killarney with moss the second time?" asked I.

"I did indeed," said she. "I went the next week, and I met a woman on the road, a cousin of John Driscoll's."

"You told me," said I, "that you and Peggy Driscoll laid out John on the table; that he was stiff and cold, a real corpse. How, then, could he rise up and run with a pike at his wife and the young farmer?"

"It was that that frightened me," said Mrs. Doyle; "but this woman told me everything. John Driscoll had a twin brother Daniel, and the two were so much alike that no man could tell one from the other. Peggy, John's wife, was from a distant parish, and she didn't know that Daniel was in the world at all. She was married to John only six months. The day that I was passing Peggy was away with a sick woman, a neighbour, from the morning till the middle of the afternoon. While she was gone Daniel came to see his brother for the first time since his marriage. He wasn't two hours in the house when he died in one minute, as if something pricked his heart. It was then that John planned to make a trial of Peggy. So he put his own clothes on Daniel, and laid the corpse on the bed above in the room and hid under the bed himself. Peggy put Daniel on the table, thinking that it was her own husband she was laying out. While Peggy was gone for the young farmer, and I was in the kitchen, John put the corpse under the bed and went on the table himself. You have the whole story now."

"I suppose you can tell me a story now with a real ghost in it," remarked I.

"Indeed, then, I can," said the old woman, "and a true story, too. I didn't know John Doyle myself nor his son, for they lived across the mountains from us, and John Doyle died a few months after my marriage, but my husband told me all about John and his son, and my husband was a man who wouldn't tell a lie, God rest his soul."

Pat Doyle and the Ghost

THERE was a young man in the next parish whose name was Pat Doyle, and one night he had to bring the priest to his father, John Doyle. It was late when the young man came to the priest's house. He knocked; a servant opened and asked what he wanted.

"The priest, for my father is dying," said Pat.

"I'll not go at this hour," said the priest; "why didn't you come earlier?"

"My father wasn't in danger till night, and besides I was work-ing far from home; I couldn't come a minute sooner."

The priest was vexed, but he mounted his horse and started. Pat Doyle and the clerk walked behind him. About half-way they came to a house where whiskey was kept, though people didn't know it generally.

"Will you wait for me here, Father?" asked Pat Doyle.

"I will," said the priest, "but don't keep me waiting too long."

Pat was barely inside when a ghost appeared behind the priest and the clerk. The priest turned, and holding the crucifix toward the ghost, spoke and held him back.

"Let us be going on," said the clerk, "the young man can come up with us."

The priest and his clerk hurried away. When Pat Doyle came out he saw neither priest nor clerk, and ran on after them. The road lay through boggy land, and there, to his terror, he saw a ghost coming in flames of fire. There was no escape at one side or another, and young Doyle had no steel to defend himself, so the ghost killed him there on the road.

The priest found the father alive, but stayed all night. He was too much in dread to go home. John Doyle grew better, but he was frightened when the son was not coming. He asked where was Pat. They said he'd come soon. But when he wasn't coming, the sick man begged his own brother's sons to go for him. One of them, Tim Doyle, was a very courageous young fellow, and said:

"I'll find him if he's in it. Neither ghost nor devil will keep him from me."

Tim went up to the loft, took an old sword and knocked a shower of rust from it. He went on his way then with his brother, and when they came to the boggy place they saw horses prancing and running around them and Pat racing on a grand steed.

"It is here he is," said Tim, "in place of going home to his dying father."

But when they came to where they thought they saw the horses, there was nothing before them but a ghost in flames of fire. Tim made at the ghost with the sword and said:

"Go, in the name of the devil; you will not frighten me." That moment the ghost disappeared, and Tim thought that all the stone walls for ten miles around him were tumbling, there was such a noise. They went on and soon they came to the body of Pat Doyle. They knelt down and examined it.

"If there is a breath in him, sure the priest will raise him," said Tim.

They carried Pat home on their shoulders. When they came to the house, they found him stone dead. As soon as John Doyle heard of his son's death, life left him that minute.

All blamed the priest for not staying with Pat, and the mother said:

"If you, Father, had stayed with him and held the crucifix against the ghost, my poor boy would be alive now."

Two days after this a neighbouring boy went up to a hillside where a herd of milch cows were grazing, and waited there till nightfall: as he was going home across the fields he saw three men walking, and near them something in the form of a he-goat; when they came up he saw that one of the three was Pat Doyle, the other two were boys killed by the same ghost months before.

The young fellow was not frightened; he spoke up and asked:

"Is this where you are, Pat Doyle? Sure I thought you were dead and buried."

"I am dead in this world," said Pat, "but I'm not dead in the next. I was killed by a mad ghost, and do you go now and tell the priest from me that it was the ghost that killed me. The priest was gone when I came out of the house. He might have saved me as he saved himself and the clerk, but he left me to the ghost."

The boy went to the priest and told him everything, and the priest believed him.

"My husband knew old John Doyle and Pat Doyle before he was killed, and Tim who carried Pat home. They were all blood relations of his."

"Perhaps Pat Doyle could have saved himself with a steel knife or a sword," said I.

"Oh, he could," answered the old woman; "my husband's cousin did the like one time. I will tell you how it was."

The Ghost of Sneem

S OME time after Pat Doyle was killed by the ghost, my husband, Martin Doyle, was at work on an estate at some distance from Sneem, and one evening the gentleman who employed Martin told him to go that night on an errand to Sneem.

"Well," said he, "it's too late and the road is very lonesome. There is no one to care for my mother but me, and if anything should happen to me she'd be without support. I'll go in the morning."

"That will not do," said the gentleman: "I want to send a letter, and it must be delivered to-night."

"I'll not risk it; I'll not go," said Martin.

Martin had a cousin James, who heard the conversation and, stepping up, he said, "I'll go. I am not afraid of ghost or spirit, and many a night have I spent on that road."

The gentleman thanked him and said:

"Here is a sword for you, if you need it." He gave James the letter with directions for delivering it.

James started off, and took every short cut and by-path, and when he thought he was half-way to Sneem a ghost stood before him in the road, and began to make at him. Whenever the ghost came near, James made a drive at him with the steel sword, for there is great virtue in steel, and above all in steel made by an Irish blacksmith. The ghost was darting at James, and he driving at the ghost with his sword till he came to a cross-road near Sneem. There the ghost disappeared, and James hurried on with great speed to Sneem. There he found that the gentleman who was to receive the letter had moved to a place six miles away, near Blackwater bridge, half-way between Sneem and Kenmare. The place has a very bad name to this day, and old people declare that there is no night without spirits and headless people being around Blackwater bridge. James knew what the place was, but he made up his mind to deliver the letter. When he came to the bridge and was going to cross it a ghost attacked him. This ghost had a venomous look and was stronger than the first one. He ran twice at James, who struck at him with the sword. Just then he saw a big man without a head running across the road at the other side of the bridge and up the cliff, though there was no path there. The ghost stopped attacking and ran after the headless man. James crossed the bridge and walked a little farther, when he met a stranger, and the two saluted each other and the man asked James where he lived, and he said: "I came from Drumfada." "Do you know what time it is?" asked James. "I do not; but when I was passing that house just below there the cocks were beginning to crow. Did you see anything?" "I did," said James, and he told him how the ghost attacked him and then ran away up the cliff after the headless man.

"Oh," said the stranger, "that headless body is always roaming around the bridge at night; hundreds of people have seen it. It ran up the cliff and disappeared at cock-crow, and the ghost that attacked you followed when the cocks crowed."

The stranger went on and James delivered the letter. The man who received it was very thankful and paid him well. James came home safe and sound, but he said: "I'd be a dead man this day but for the steel."

"Could you tell me a real fairy tale?" asked I of the old woman.

"I could," said she, "but to-day I'll tell you only what I saw one night beyond Cahirciveen:

Once I spent the night at a house near Waterville, about six miles from Derrynane. The woman of the house was lying in bed at the time and a young child with her. The husband heard an infant crying outside under the window, and running to the bed he said:

"Yerra, Mary, have you the child with you?"

"Indeed, then, I have, John."

"Well, I heard a child crying under the window. I'll go this minute and see whose it is."

"In the name of God," screamed the wife, "stop inside! Get the holy water and sprinkle it over the children and over me and yourself."

He did this, and then sprinkled some in the kitchen. He heard the crying go off farther and farther till it seemed half a mile away: it was very pitiful and sad. If he had gone to the door the man of the house would have got a fairy stroke and the mother would have been taken as a nurse to the fort.

This is all the old woman told. When going she promised to come on the following day, but I have not seen her since. The blind man informed me some evenings later that she was sick and in the "ashpitl" (hospital). Her sickness was caused, as she said, by telling me tales in the daytime. Many of the old people will tell tales only in the evening; it is not right, not lucky, to do so during daylight.

The Dead Mother

THE next two tales were told by the blind man whom I have mentioned in connection with fairy tales told at Ventry Strand.

It is not out of place to refer here to a certain popular error. It is supposed by many persons that women are the chief depositories of tales touching fairies and other extra-human characters, but they are not. It is a rare thing to find a woman in possession of wonderful tales of the best quality. During researches extending over a number of years, I have found among Indians in the United States only one woman who could be classed with the very best tale-tellers. In Ireland I have found few women who can tell tales at all, and none who can compare with the best men. I believe this is so in all countries.

The two following stories testify to a perfect communication at times between this world and another.

There was a girl in Cloghane whose name was Mary Shea. She married and had three children, one son and two daughters. Her husband died; then his people turned against her and began to quarrel with the widow. Mary was a quiet, good woman, and didn't like trouble. So she told her brother-in-law that if he would give her money to go to America with her two girls she would give up the bit of land that she had and leave the little boy with himself till she would send for him.

The brother-in-law and the other friends made up the money, and she went away and was doing well in America for about twelve months, and then she took a fever and died.

The very same week that the mother died the girls sent money home for their brother. They wanted to send it while the mother was sick, but they waited to know would she get better. But she died and was buried.

About two weeks after the woman's death a girl in Cloghane was going one evening to Castlegregory for sea-moss. Walking along, she saw a woman ahead, and hurried on to have company and shorten the road for herself. The woman ahead seemed in no hurry and waited.

The girl spoke, and as they walked along the woman asked where was she going, and she told her. "Do you know me?" asked the woman.

"I do not," said the girl, "but I think I have seen you."

"Didn't you know Mary Fitzgerald?"

"Oh, I did; and when did you come home?"

"About two weeks ago."

"Isn't it the wonder that your mother in Cloghane doesn't know you are here?"

"I was in Cloghane," said she, "and saw them all, and 'tis badly they are treating my little boy, but 'twill not be long that way; he will go to his sisters in America. I died two weeks ago, but don't be in dread of me, for I'll do you no harm. I wanted you to speak to me, so I could tell you what to do. When you go home tomorrow go to my mother and tell her that I died in America, and that you saw me on this strand, that I am walking back and forth perishing with the cold. Tell her to buy a pair of shoes and stockings and give them to some poor person in my name, for God's sake."

Mary was talking a long time to the girl, and the girl promised to go to the mother.

It seems that whatever Mary's son did his uncle whipped him, and the boy was crying in the daytime and crying at night in bed, the night that Mary came first to Cloghane. Everybody in the house was silent except the boy, and he was crying. The mother walked in, bent over him, laid her hand on his shoulder and said,

"Don't be crying, my poor little boy, you'll be with your sisters very soon. You'll not see your mother any more, but you'll be happy without her."

He sat up in the bed, knew her, and grasping at her let such a screech out of him that it roused the uncle and grandmother, and he told them what he'd seen.

Next day a letter came from America with news of the mother's death. Just after the girl came to the house and was telling about the shoes, the letter was brought in.

The mother bought a pair of shoes and gave them to a poor woman, for God's sake and the good of Mary's soul, and Mary was seen on the strand no more after that.

Tim Sheehy Sent Back to This World to Prove His Innocence
(told by William Keating)

THERE was a farmer, fourteen miles from Tralee, named Fitzgerald, who, by sly management and being a spy on his neighbours, became a great friend of the landlord. He carried matters that far that at last he got enough small tenants ejected to give him the grass of forty cows. Within his bounds was a sub-tenant of the name of Tim Sheehy, and Fitzgerald was very anxious to have this man ejected. He made complaints to the landlord. He said Sheehy was poaching and destroying game, and said this and that of him.

The landlord didn't believe these complaints, for Sheehy and his father before him were honest men, who paid their rent always. At last, by some chance, Fitzgerald's cow-house was burned down one night and ten cows were destroyed in the fire. A great many suspected Tim Sheehy. What they said was that Tim owed Fitzgerald a spite, and sure who else would be burning the cow-house? Fitzgerald was only too willing to take up the story and spread it.

There was a woman in the village by the name of Kate Pendy, who had her own opinion, and she gave it:

"Wisha, then, a ghraghil,"° said she to a friend. "Tim Sheehy is as clear of that as God Himself. There is no fear that that poor, honest man burned the cow-house."

This was Saturday, and Tim Sheehy was in Tralee on some business that he had, and he didn't come home till the following morning. When he was nearing the chapel and mass just over, crowds were around, and he heard a man say: "There goes Tim Sheehy, who burned Fitzgerald's cow-house and ran away: I wonder what's bringing him back?"

"Sure, 'tis the finger of God," said a second man. "The Lord wouldn't let another be punished in place of him."

Sheehy hung his head and was cut to the heart at these words. He went home, and whether it was from grief or sickness that he died, 'twas unknown, but he died that very day. When he was washed and ready to be laid on the table the wife sent to a neighbouring woman, a cousin of Fitzgerald, for the loan of sheets to hang over the table and the corpse. The woman refused to lend the sheets. "I'll not give them," said she; "the divil mend Sheehy, he ruined my poor cousin."

The boy went home without the sheets, and Mrs. Sheehy found them at another house. A deal of people met at the wake house; they sat down and began to smoke and tell stories, as people do always at wakes. What was their surprise at midnight when Tim Sheehy sat up on the table and began to speak to them.

"Friends and neighbours," said he, "ye needn't be in dread of me; I'll not harm any person here present. It wasn't I that burned the cow-house. The man who did that is beyond the mountain at this time. People broke my heart, killed me with false accusations, but I got leave to return and tell you of my innocence and take the stain from my children." Sheehy was talking on, and would have said a deal more but for an old woman, Nancy Brady, who was sitting in the corner, and a wide ruffled white cap on her. She rose up. "Tim, my darling," said she, "did you see my mother?"

Sheehy looked at her fiercely. "Bad luck to you, you hag," said he, "I did, and she is now what she was in life, a tale-bearing disturber, and dishonest. She goes about milking the neighbours'

°Gradhghil, voc. of gradhgeal, white love, darling.

cows when she thinks nobody is looking at her, just as she used to do in this world." Tim Sheehy turned then to the people: "I can say no more, as I was interrupted by this woman." With that he dropped back dead and speechless.

All the people in it were cursing Nancy Brady because she wouldn't stop quiet till they could hear what Tim Sheehy had to tell about the other world.

Tom Moore and the Seal Woman

A PROPOS of the following tale, I may say: The intermarriage with and descent of men from beings not human touches upon one of the most interesting and important points in primitive belief. Totemism among savage races in our day, and descent from the gods in antiquity, are the best examples of this belief; derived from it, in all probability, but remotely, are family escutcheons with their animals and birds and the emblematic beasts and birds of nations, such as the Roman eagle, the British lion, the American eagle, the Russian bear. The Roman eagle and the wolf which suckled Romulus may have been totems, if not for the Romans, at least for some earlier people. The lion, eagle, and bear of England, America, and Russia are of course not totemic, though adopted in imitation of people who, if they had not totems, had as national emblems birds or beasts that at some previous period were real totems for some social body.

There is a tale in Scotland concerning people of the clan MacCodrum, who were seals in the daytime, but men and women at night. No man of the MacCodrums, it is said, would kill a seal. The MacCodrums are mentioned in Gaelic as "Clann Mhic Codruim nan rón" (Clan MacCodrum of the seals).

In the village of Kilshanig, two miles north-east of Castlegregory, there lived at one time a fine, brave young man named Tom Moore, a good dancer and singer. 'Tis often he was heard singing among the cliffs and in the fields of a night.

Tom's father and mother died and he was alone in the house and in need of a wife. One morning early, when he was at work near the strand, he saw the finest woman ever seen in that part of the kingdom, sitting on a rock, fast asleep. The tide was gone from the rocks then, and Tom was curious to know who was she or what brought her, so he walked toward the rock.

"Wake up!" cried Tom to the woman; "if the tide comes 'twill drown you."

She raised her head and only laughed. Tom left her there, but as he was going he turned every minute to look at the woman. When he came back he caught the spade, but couldn't work; he had to look at the beautiful woman on the rock. At last the tide swept over the rock. He threw the spade down and away to the strand with him, but she slipped into the sea and he saw no more of her that time.

Tom spent the day cursing himself for not taking the woman from the rock when it was God that sent her to him. He couldn't work out the day. He went home.

Tom could not sleep a wink all that night. He was up early next morning and went to the rock. The woman was there. He called to her.

No answer. He went up to the rock. "You may as well come home with me now," said Tom. Not a word from the woman. Tom took the hood from her head and said, "I'll have this!"

The moment he did that she cried: "Give back my hood, Tom Moore!"

"Indeed I will not, for 'twas God sent you to me, and now that you have speech I'm well satisfied! And taking her by the arm he led her to the house. The woman cooked breakfast, and they sat down together to eat it.

"Now," said Tom, "in the name of God you and I'll go to the priest and get married, for the neighbours around here are very watchful; they'd be talking." So after breakfast they went to the priest, and Tom asked him to marry them.

"Where did you get the wife?" asked the priest.

Tom told the whole story. When the priest saw Tom was so anxious to marry he charged £5, and Tom paid the money. He took the wife home with him, and she was as good a woman as ever went into a man's house. She lived with Tom seven years, and had three sons and two daughters.

One day Tom was ploughing, and some part of the plough rigging broke. He thought there were bolts on the loft at home, so he climbed up to get them. He threw down bags and ropes while he was looking for the bolts, and what should he throw down but the hood which he took from the wife seven years before. She saw it the moment it fell, picked it up, and hid it. At that time people heard a great seal roaring out in the sea.

"Ah," said Tom's wife, "that's my brother looking for me."

Some men who were hunting killed three seals that day. All the women of the village ran down to the strand to look at the seals, and Tom's wife with the others. She began to moan, and going up to the dead seals she spoke some words to each and then cried out, "Oh, the murder!"

When they saw her crying the men said: "We'll have nothing more to do with these seals." So they dug a great hole, and the three seals were put into it and covered. But some thought in the night: "'Tis a great shame to bury those seals, after all the trouble in taking them." Those men went with shovels and dug up the earth, but found no trace of the seals.

All this time the big seal in the sea was roaring. Next day when Tom was at work his wife swept the house, put everything in order, washed the children and combed their hair; then, taking them one by one, she kissed each. She went next to the rock, and, putting the hood on her head, gave a plunge. That moment the big seal rose and roared so that people ten miles away could hear him.

Tom's wife went away with the seal swimming in the sea. All the five children that she left had webs between their fingers and toes, half-way to the tips.

The descendants of Tom Moore and the seal woman are living near Castlegregory to this day, and the webs are not gone yet from between their fingers and toes, though decreasing with each generation.

The Four-Leafed Shamrock

THIS tale gives a good instance of the virtue of the four-leafed shamrock against the power which takes people's eyes—*i.e.*, true vision—from them:

A good many years ago a showman came to the town of Dingle and performed many tricks there. At one time he'd eat a dozen straws and then pull yards of ribbon from his throat. The strangest thing he showed was a game-cock that he used to harness to a great log of wood.

Men, women, and children were breaking their bones, running to see the cock, and he a small bird, drawing such a great weight of timber. One day, when the showman was driving the cock on the road toward Brandon Mountain, he met a man with a bundle of fresh grass on his back. The man was astonished to see crowds running after a cock dragging one straw behind him.

"You fool," said the people, "don't you see the cock drawing a log of timber, and it would fail any horse to draw the like of it?"

"Indeed, then, I do not. I see the cock dragging a straw behind him, and sure I've seen the like many a time in my own place."

Hearing this, the showman knew that there was something in the grass, and going over to the man he asked what price was he asking for the bundle. The man didn't wish to sell the grass, but at last he parted with it for eighteen pence. The showman gave the grass to his boy and told him to go aside and drop it into the river. The boy did that, and when the bundle went down with the stream the man was as big a fool as another; he ran after the cock with the crowd.

That evening the same man was telling a friend how at first he saw the cock with a straw behind him, and then saw him drawing a great log of wood. "Oh, you fool!" said the friend, "there was a four-leafed shamrock in your bundle of grass; while you had the shamrock it kept every enchantment and devilment from you, and when you parted with it, you became as big a fool as the others."

The burial customs of Ireland are very interesting because they throw light on beliefs concerning another life—beliefs that were once universal on the island and are held yet in a certain way by a good many people. There is much variety in the burial customs of the whole country, but I can refer only to one or two details which are observed carefully in the peninsula west of Killarney.

When the coffin is ready to be taken to the grave the lid is nailed down, but when it is at the edge of the grave the nails are drawn and placed one across another on the lid, which is left unfastened.

In arranging the corpse in the coffin the feet are generally fastened together to keep them in position. This is done frequently by pinning the stockings to each other; but however done, the fastening is removed before burial and the feet are left perfectly free. The corpse is not bound in any way or confined in the coffin. That it is held necessary to free the feet of the corpse is shown by what happened once in Cahirciveen. A man died and his widow forgot to remove the pins fastening his stockings to each other. The voice of the dead man came to the woman on the night after the funeral, telling her that his feet were bound, and to free them. Next day she had the grave opened, took the pins from the stockings, and left the feet untrammelled.

It is believed as firmly by some people that the dead rise from their graves time after time, each by himself independently, as it is by others that all men will rise ages hence at one call and be judged for their deeds simultaneously. Besides the separate movements of each dead person we have the great social apparition on the night of All Saints, when the dead come to the houses of their friends and sit by the fire, unseen of all save those who are to die within the coming year. In view of this visit a good fire is made, the room is swept carefully, and prayers are repeated.

When I inquired why the nails were drawn from the coffin and bonds removed from the corpse with such care, some persons said that it was an old superstition, others that it was an old custom, and others still that it was done to give the dead man his freedom.

In the following tale, that relating to John Cokeley, we have a good instance of punishment by fairies. The head and front of John's offending was that he stopped the passage against the fairies. The first result of that act was a slight attack of illness, the second his removal to another world, which, though invisible to all between sunrise and sunset, and visible between sunset and sunrise to few only, is right here on earth. Cokeley's place in the house is held by a fairy substitute with a ravenous appetite, a sour temper, and a sharp tongue, the usual qualities of such an agent.

I know one old man who has an afflicted daughter, and who

believes firmly that she has been put in his house by the fairies; he thinks that his own daughter was taken away and this creature given to him. This one has the "tongue of an attorney," while his daughter was a "quiet, honest girl."

The crowning proofs that Cokeley was taken by the fairies are that he was seen repeatedly after sunset, and the sick man refused before his death to see the priest.

In the tale of Tom Foley there is no real ghost, but there is strong evidence of a general and firm belief that ghosts go among men and are active on earth.

John Cokeley and the Fairy

THERE was a farmer in the parish of Firez whose name was John Cokeley. John was a great man for every kind of new information, and would go a long way of an evening to hear people read newspapers, but he didn't give in to stories or to what old people used to say.

Cokeley thought the house he had too small and wanted to put an addition to it. There was an old passage at one end of the house, and it's there he was going to build the addition. John had a gossip who used to go with the fairies, and this man passed the way when he was beginning the work.

"What's that you are doing?" asked the gossip.

"Don't you see what I am doing?" said Cokeley.

"Couldn't you put the addition to the other end of the house and leave this one alone?"

"That wouldn't suit me," answered John.

"You should leave the passage open so that every one could travel through it by day, and especially by night."

"That's foolish talk," said Cokeley.

"Very well," said the gossip, "you think so I suppose, but my word for it, you may be sorry in the end."

Cokeley finished the addition, and left a little hole in the wall near the fireplace, and it was there he kept his pipe and tobacco. One night on going to bed he put an ounce of tobacco in the hole (there was no one smoking in the house but himself). In the morning there was no bit of the tobacco left, but in place of it the price, three-pence-ha'penny. He took great notice of that. A few weeks later he rose from his bed in the night and heard a great noise of horsemen outside. He opened the door and looked out, but if he did he saw nothing. He went to bed again, and wasn't long there when he began to be sore and feel very sick in himself. The gossip came to see him next day: "Well, John," said he, "you feel sick to-day."

"I do," said Cokeley.

"You had a right to stop in bed."

"How well you know of that," said Cokeley.

"I do; that much could not be done unknown to me. When you turned back from the door last night there was a crowd between you and the bed as big as at any fair. They gave you only a warning this time, and you'll recover."

In a few weeks' time Cokeley was looking well again, but he got downhearted, took to drinking, and spent his means, so that at last he hadn't any cows on his land but what belonged to others. One May-day in the evening he was going to a neighbour's to collect grazing money that was due to him. When about three-quarters of the way—and the time was after sunset—a woman appeared opposite and took a great fall out of him. He was thrown on his face in the middle of the road and struck senseless. In half an hour he recovered, rose, and walked on; after going a short distance he was knocked a second time, and soon after he got the third fall. Cokeley didn't know for a full hour where he was; he hadn't his senses. When he came to himself he was in the middle of the road; he crawled to the side of it, then rose and went for his money. He didn't tell the man what had happened, made no delay, but hurried home and went to bed. He felt the strength parting from his body in the night, and was without any power to move next morning. His wife ran to doctors for cures, but no use for her. In a month's time all the neighbours said that Cokeley was fairy struck, and there was no cure. The wife went one day to Killarney, where she met the gossip.

"John is very bad again," said the gossip.

"He is," said she. "There is no one to do good for him if you don't."

"Oh, well," said the gossip, "I have a son of my own to assist, and he is nearer to me than what John is; I must look out for myself. John was struck very severely, and he may thank himself for it. He was not said by me, or he wouldn't have built in the passage, and wouldn't be where he is to-day. This is all the cure I can give you: Go home, get a tub of water, and bathe John nine nights with the one water, one night after another. When you have that done you'll not throw out the water till after midnight, when all are in bed. Take care that no one of your family is out of the house that night."

When John's wife was in the road coming home a man of the neighbours overtook her and they walked on together. There was a height within one mile of the house; from this they had a fine view of Cokeley's house and land—the time was after sunset—and to their surprise they saw John himself walking around in the garden as well and strong as ever, but when the wife came home she found him in bed, sick and miserable.

"Were you out since morning, John?" asked she.

He only began to scold and look bitter at her. "How could a dead man leave the bed?" said he.

She prepared the tub of water in the corner of the house that day, and was bathing him for nine nights in the same water. She had a son fifteen or sixteen years of age who wasn't at home. He spent a night out very often, for he was working for people. She didn't think the boy would come that time, it was so late (about one o'clock in the morning). She began to throw out the water with a gallon.* There was a big flag† outside the door; she threw the water on that. She had all out but the last gallon, when who should come but the son. When he stepped on the flag he was thrown heels over head and his leg broken. There was no doctor nearer than Killarney. When the mother went there next day she met the gossip.

"Well," said he, "you are worse now than ever. Didn't I tell

---

*A vessel for dipping water; it holds a few quarts.   †A flagstone.

you not to throw out that water when there was any one away from the house?"

"He slept out so often," said the mother, "that I was sure he wouldn't come that night."

"You may thank your friends and neighbours [of the other world] for being so strong, or your son's brains would be knocked out on that flag. He'll not be long recovering. The washing did no good to John, but he'll not leave you yet; he's very far back in the ranks. He will not go from you till he'll be the front man. Don't take too much care of him; he'll rob you."

When a neighbour came in the sick man had a tongue for any attorney, complaining of the wife, saying that she was only starving him. He would eat nothing from the poor woman but the best meat, butter and eggs; he should get a pint of whiskey every day. Every day he should be placed in a chair and brought to the fire between two persons. By looking at him you'd think there was nothing amiss with the man; besides, he had such an appetite and such a tongue for talking.

Soon the neighbours stopped coming, and didn't inquire. They used to see John Cokeley walking about the farm after sunset and before sunrise; they thought he was well again. This went on about four years, and the gossip who used to be with the fairies left this world altogether.

In the latter end the wife couldn't give the sick man what food he wanted, and he was raging; he kept the appetite all the time. She had a third cousin, a priest, and the priest came to see her.

"Oh, father, can't you do some good for my husband? Myself and my poor children are beggared from him."

"It isn't in my power to do good to that man," said the priest. "You must leave him there till he is taken from you."

She told how the husband abused her, what a tongue he had.

"Don't give him another tint of whiskey," said the priest, "nor meat, nor eggs. Give him what you and your children have."

The man gave a bitter look at the priest. The priest gave a good morning and went home. After this the poor woman put no food before him but such as she and the children used. He was pining away and hadn't half the speech he had before, but he called her all the names he could think of. If he could have killed her he would.

It continued on in this way till one month before seven years were out, he pining, she breaking her heart with poverty.

This month he was sleeping all the time. They knew there was a change coming.

One midnight they heard a great crowd racing around the house, a noise of horses and people about the cross-road, and hurricanes of wind with terrible noises.

"Ah, I'll be going home soon," said he on the following morning. "I'm not sorry to leave you."

"Would you like to have a priest, John?" asked the wife.

"What would I do with a priest, woman?"

The uproar continued three nights. On the third evening he asked to eat—said he was starved. She gave him plenty of what she had and he ate willingly, without any word at all from him. Herself and son and the little family, five altogether, were talking, and in an hour's time, when they didn't hear any sound from him, they went to the bed and found that it's dead he was, and they were not sorry after him; and sure why should they, for it wasn't John Cokeley that was in it at all.

Tom Foley's Ghost

THERE was a man Tom Foley, a farmer who lived at Castle-main, near the Leann River; he had a brother John, who lived eight miles beyond Tralee, on a farm of his own which he had there. The Leann is a great river for fishing; above all, when the weather is favourable.

Tom Foley went fishing once on a cloudy day when it was raining a little. There was a great rise of fish in the river, and Tom was killing a power of them that turn.

The place where Tom was fishing was about seven fields from his house without being in sight of it. The main road was very near the river, and Tom wasn't above an hour killing fish when a man came the way on horseback, and when he saw Foley on the bank he made toward him.

"Is your name Tom Foley?" asked the man.

"It is," said Tom.

"Have you a brother named John?"

"I have."

"Well, your brother is dead; he got a sudden death yesterday. I am his servant man, and I was sent by John's wife to say that you are wanted at the house without delay."

"You'd better not go back to-day," said Tom to the man. "There is a great rise of fish in this river; I haven't seen the like since I was born. Stop fishing here after me; you'll have time enough for the funeral to-morrow."

"Leave your overcoat with me," said the man, "and I'll stop."

Tom gave his overcoat to the man and said, "I'll not mind going home. The clothes I have on will do very well, and do you take what fish I killed and what you'll kill yourself to my house: you'll find the road to it easily."

Tom mounted his horse and rode off. The servant man, who was of Tom's size, put on the coat and was fishing away for a few hours, when, whatever way it happened, he fell into the river and was drowned.

There were two other fishermen on the bank of the river at a distance from Tom. They didn't see the horse coming nor the servant man changing places with Foley, and they thought it was Tom was in it all the time. After a while they looked again, but if they did, they got no sight of a man on the bank.

"It seems Tom has gone home," said one of the men; "there is no rise of fish here, and I'll go fishing the river down before me."

He went down till he came to where Foley's bag of fish was. He knew then that it was not home he went. So he looked into the water, and what should he see but the body at the bottom of the river and Tom Foley's coat on it. He screeched out to the other man then, saying that Tom Foley was drowned.

The other man came and stayed in the place, while the first went with an account to the house and told Tom's wife, Mary, that her husband was drowned in the river. Mary began to screech and lament in a way you'd think the life would leave her. The man ran and collected the neighbours, and went with them and Mary Foley to bring home the corpse.

When the people raised the body from the river, they found the face all eaten by eels: no one could know that it was Tom Foley was in it but for the coat.

Mary began to moan and lament now at sight of the body. "Oh," cried she, "Tom aghraghil, you're gone from me; how can I live without you now? Oh, Tom, my darling, why did you leave me?"

It would bring the tears to any man's eyes to look at poor Mary Foley, and her heart nearly breaking. The neighbours took the body home, and there was a great wake in the Foleys' house that night. The neighbouring women comforted Mary the best way they could.

"Don't be flying in the face of God, my dear," said one old woman; "sure nothing happens in the whole world without the will of the Almighty. It was the Lord took your husband, and you should bear the loss and be resigned; the Lord will reward you."

Next day there was a great funeral, for Tom had many friends and relations. The parish priest himself went to the funeral; he didn't send the curate.

The graveyard was four miles from Tom's village, and on the road home Mary Foley and her three brothers stopped at a public-house, half-way. They were tired, hungry, and dry; in need of refreshment. Mary's brothers had a friend of theirs with them, a man who lived two villages away—a fine, able, strong fellow, and he sat down with the company.

When they had eaten a bite and taken some drink for themselves, Mary was complaining of her lonely condition, and the tears coming out of her eyes. "How am I to live without Tom?" asked she. "Sure everybody will be robbing me. I'll be beggared unless ye do something to help me."

"Yerra, woman, how are we to help you?" said the oldest brother. "We have all we can do to mind our own families."

"That's true for you," said the second brother, "but still and all we can mend the trouble. There is no way for you, Mary," said he, turning to the sister, "but to marry, and the sooner you marry the better. Servant-men will neglect your work; they'll only be taking your money, and eating and drinking all before them. It's not long you'll have a roof over your head, if it's depending on servant-men you'll be. You must marry, and the sooner the better."

With that the company had another glass.

"Now, Mary," said the brother, "here is the man for you to marry—John Garvey, a friend of mine, and you couldn't find a better husband if you were to wait ten years for him."

Mary started up against the brother, and wasn't it a shame for him, she said, to be scandalising her with his talk, and wouldn't it be fitter for him to have some respect for his only sister. The other brothers helped this one now, and the end of the whole matter was that before they left the public-house the match was made between John Garvey and Mary.

"Follow my advice, Mary," said the eldest brother; "go straight to the priest's house and be married offhand; sure there's no good in waiting."

"Wouldn't it be a shame before all the neighbours for me to marry on the day of my first husband's funeral?"

"Sure the neighbours needn't know that you are married. Let them think that John is in service with you."

"The priest wouldn't marry us," said Mary, "if we asked him."

"Believe me, he'll marry you if you pay him well," said the brother.

Whether in her heart Mary was willing or not, no one knew, but she consented. "Have no fear," said the brothers; "no one will know anything of the marriage but the priest and ourselves."

They went to the priest's house, and when all were inside, the servant-girl went up to the priest and said that Mrs. Foley was below in the kitchen. The priest came. He said he was very sorry for her loss, and asked what could he do for her? what was it brought her?

"Oh, father," said she, "I am in a very bad way as I am. Every one will be striving to rob me, and nobody to do my work. My brothers tell me that if I'll be said by them I'll marry, and I'm thinking to follow their advice, and it's that that brought me."

"Oh, you villain of a woman, to marry a second time on the day of your first husband's funeral!"

"Don't blame me, father," said Mary; "maybe you'd have another mind from what you have if you were in my place. Sure no one need be the wiser. Marry me to this man here, John Garvey, and I'll give you three pounds."

"I will not take it from you," said the priest.

"Well, father, I'll give you all the money I have in my pocket: I'll give you five pounds."

"I'll not marry you," said the priest.

With that, one of the brothers took Mary aside and said: "Say that you'll give him the big pig you have as well as the money."

"Well, father," said Mary, "with the five pounds I'll give you a fat pig that'll keep you in bacon for a twelvemonth."

Now one of the brothers spoke up: "There is no need of publishing the marriage at present. People will think that John Garvey is in service with my sister."

The priest wanted to refuse, and was opening his mouth, but the first word wasn't out when the curate took him aside and said:

"Why not marry the poor woman? Marry her. No one will be the worse for it, and no one the wiser; and, besides, you'll have a supply of fine bacon."

The priest consented at last. One of the brothers and the priest's own servant-girl were the witnesses, and nobody knew a word of what happened. Mary Foley that was—she was Mary Garvey now—paid the five pounds, left good health with the priest, and was thankful to him. Herself and her new husband went home and the brothers went to their own houses. There was no one before the young couple but the servant-girl and Tom Foley's mother. The old woman was surprised when she saw John Garvey, and wondered what brought him on the evening of Tom's funeral.

Mary sent the servant-girl about a mile away on an errand, and when the girl was gone she turned to Garvey and said:

"Well, John, bring your sister to-morrow to work for me, and I'll not delay you any longer."

With that John turned away and Mary went with Foley's mother to an outhouse. While they were gone, Garvey went back, walked into his wife's room, shut the door, and stopped inside. After a time the servant girl came home and went to bed in her own place, and the poor old mother was left alone at the hearth, lamenting and mourning for her son dead and buried.

When the light was out and all was still and quiet, about ten o'clock, Tom Foley came home, after burying his brother. He tried to open the door. It was bolted; he knocked. The mother went to the door, and when she heard Tom's voice she was frightened and asked what was troubling his soul, that he'd come back from the other world after being buried that day.

"Oh, mother," said Foley, "open the door and leave me in."

"I will not," said the mother. "You cannot come in, my son; but tell me what is troubling your soul. I'll have masses said for you and give alms."

Foley was very tired after the journey, and couldn't stop at the door any longer. He went to the barn; there was a large heap of straw in one end of it, and four or five pigs with the big pig at the other end. Foley lay down in the straw and soon he was asleep.

During the evening the parish priest began to be in dread that the woman might change her mind; now that she was married she might put the pig aside and he'd be left without his bacon. So he called his servant-boy and told him to bring the big pig from Mrs. Foley's.

The boy took a whip and went to Tom's house for the pig. He knew well where was the barn and where was the pig. When he came to the barn he went in and stirred up the pigs; they began to screech and make a great noise. The big pig being so bulky and strong, wouldn't go out, and Foley woke up with the screeching. He looked around to know what was troubling the pigs, and saw the boy striving to take the big one away with him. Tom was in very bad humour, so he made after the boy and gave him a good blow in the back with a wattle, and asked, is it stealing he was at that hour of the night?

The boy was knocked, but if he was, he rose quickly and away with him like the wind. He didn't get another blow, though he had three or four falls from fright before he reached the priest's house, thinking that Foley was after him. When he went in there was terror in his heart. The priest asked, did he bring the pig so soon? He said he didn't bring the pig, and he couldn't, for Tom Foley was minding the place as well as if he wasn't buried at all.

"What's that you tell me?" asked the priest.

"Oh, father, sure when I went to bring the pig Tom Foley was inside in the straw. The pigs made a noise, and he ran after me with a big wattle and asked why was I disturbing his pigs at that hour of the night. He gave me a blow in the back and knocked me on the road. I got three or four other falls from fright before I came home."

"Yerra, go, my boy, and bring me the pig. It's some stranger that's in it; it's thieving he is. If you don't bring the pig to-night, maybe we won't have him to bring on Monday."

"Whatever you do, father, or whatever will happen to the pig, I won't face Foley a second time," said the boy.

The priest called a small boy that he had herding, and said, "Go you and bring the big pig from Foley's."

"I'll go if somebody goes with me."

"Oh, I'll go with him," said the curate's brother, who happened to be visiting him. "I know the place, and I knew Tom Foley."

The two went off together, and the curate's brother stopped a couple of fields away from Foley's house. The boy went on, and when he began to drive out the big pig, the pig made a noise that woke Foley a second time, and he went after this boy more venomously than after the first one. The boy ran for his life to the field where the curate's brother was. Foley had to turn back, and didn't catch him. The curate's brother saw Foley hunting the boy, and knew that 'twas no lie for the first boy, that the ghost was in it. The two hurried home with what strength was in their legs.

"Oh, then, Foley's ghost is there as sure as I am standing before you," said the brother to the curate in presence of the priest.

On the following morning Foley rose out of the barn drowsy and queer after the night. The door of his house was closed and he had no chance of going in. "I will go to first mass," thought Tom, "with the clothes I have on; Mary will be up before me when I come home. I can sleep the remainder of the day and take a good rest."

Whenever a man going the way saw Foley he left the road to

him and ran through the field. Foley didn't know why people were leaving the road to him. When he went into the chapel all made a rush towards the altar. The priest, who came out at the moment, asked the people what ailed them.

"Oh, God between us and harm," said one, "Tom Foley is here from the other world."

The priest called Foley by name, and asked, was he there?

"Why shouldn't I be here, father? Don't you see me?"

"Tell me, in the name of God, where did you come from?" asked the priest.

"Where would I come from," said Foley, "but from my own house?"

"Sure the whole parish knows that you were drowned," said the priest, "and buried yesterday. Wasn't I at your funeral myself?"

"Well, then, you and the whole parish were mistaken," said Foley. "I buried my brother John yesterday eight miles beyond Tralee."

"And who was the man that was drowned?" asked the priest.

"I left my brother's servant-man here fishing instead of myself. Maybe he was drowned and the people buried him. I know well that they didn't bury me."

The priest stepped out and called the curate, and told him that Foley wasn't dead at all. "Do you hurry now to Tom's house," said he, "and tell John Garvey to be off with himself, that Foley is alive and will be home very soon, and when Garvey is gone tell Mrs. Foley that I'll come with Tom after first mass, and to be ready for him."

The curate hurried away, and the priest went in to Foley. "Your wife may not believe that you are not dead," said he. "I will go with you after mass and tell her that you are not dead at all."

"I knew," said Tom, "that there was something wrong. It was late last night when I came home. My wife was in bed, no one up before me but my mother, and she wouldn't open the door for me, but began to ask what was troubling my soul. She said to tell her, and she would give alms and have mass said for me. Now I know why this was."

"It will be the same with her to-day," said the priest. "I'll go to the house with you."

The two went to the house after mass. When Mary Foley saw Tom she dropped on the bench and looked as though she'd die from fright.

"Don't be afraid," said the priest. "It wasn't Tom that was buried but his brother's servant-man."

Tom told the wife how he gave the loan of his coat to the servant-man and went to bury his brother John. The wife was satisfied now. The priest took her aside, and told her to have no trouble of mind on account of what she had done by getting married.

"You meant no harm," said he, "but no one in the world must know a word about it. You and I will keep our own—do you keep the big pig and I'll keep my five pounds."

The following curious story reminds one a little of Slavic tales of dead men who dwell in their tombs as in houses. Some of the Slav tomb-dwellers are harmless, others malignant. The malignant ones are dead persons who rise up bodily and go around at night devouring people. When one of these has eaten a victim he rushes back to his grave, for he is obliged to remain wherever he may be at cock-crow; if outside his grave, he falls stiff and helpless to lie there till the next night. There are two ways of giving a quietus to such a ghoul. One is to pin him to the earth by driving a stake of aspen wood through his heart; the other is to burn him to ashes. The burning, as described in Russian tales, is performed by a great crowd of people armed with bushes, long brooms, shovels, and rakes. These gather round the fire to drive back everything that comes from the body. When the body is on the fire a short time it bursts, and a whole legion of devilry rush forth in the form of worms, snakes, bats, beetles, flies, birds; these try with all their might to get away. Each carries the fate of the ghoul with it. If only one of them escapes, the dead man will be eating people the next night as actively as ever, but if the crowd drive every thing into the fire again he will be destroyed utterly.

A striking trait in the Irish fairy tales is the number of

observances caused by the presence of fairies, rules of ordinary living, so to speak. For instance, nothing is more pleasing to fairies than a well-swept kitchen and clean water. A dirty kitchen and foul water bring their resentment.

The ghosts or night-walking dead, as they belong to the other world, seem to have at least in some cases the same likes and dislikes as the fairies. In the following tale Michael Derrihy, the dead man brought from the tomb by Kate, kills the three brothers because the people in the house did not throw out dirty water and brought in none that was clean, and he is determined that they shall stay killed, for he tries to do away with the only cure that can bring them to life again. Various acts of personal uncleanliness involve punishment from the fairies. In one tale they carry off from a mother an infant which she fails to wash properly; in another a careless, untidy girl, who rises in the night and commits offensive acts in the kitchen, is punished in a signal manner. There is present a whole party of fairies, men and women, though unseen by the girl. One of the women, who is making tea, takes a saucer and hurls it at her as she is returning to bed. The saucer is broken; one half flies over the bed to the wall beyond, the other is buried in the girl's hip. She screams and wakes the whole house. No one can help her. She is in bed for three years after that in great suffering. No relief for her till her mother, who had just earned the gratitude of the fairies by acts of service, prays to have her daughter cured.

The fairy woman tells how the daughter offended and how she was punished, says that if the mother will go to the wall she will find one half of the saucer there; if she applies that to the affected part of the daughter's body it will cure her. The mother does as directed. One half of the saucer comes out of the hip to join the other, and the girl is cured straightway.

When the fairies are maltreated or despised they take ample vengeance; they punish severely. They are generous in a like degree for services or acts of kindness. So far as fairy methods of action are revealed to us in tales and popular beliefs, they constitute a system of rewards and punishments regulating the intercourse between this world and another. They are parts of an early religion in which material services are rewarded by material benefits, and in which conduct bordering upon morality is inculcated.

The ghosts, mainly malignant and nearly all women, are represented as partly under fairy rules and partly under Church punishment. Their position is not fixed so definitely.

The Blood-Drawing Ghost

THERE was a young man in the parish of Drimalegue, county Cork, who was courting three girls at one time, and he didn't know which of them would he take; they had equal fortunes, and any of the three was as pleasing to him as any other. One day when he was coming home from the fair with his two sisters, the sisters began:

"Well, John," said one of them, "why don't you get married. Why don't you take either Mary, or Peggy, or Kate?"

"I can't tell you that," said John, "till I find which of them has the best wish for me."

"How will you know?" asked the other.

"I will tell you that as soon as any person will die in the parish."

In three weeks' time from that day an old man died. John went to the wake and then to the funeral. While they were burying the corpse in the graveyard John stood near a tomb which was next to the grave, and when all were going away, after burying the old man, he remained standing a while by himself, as if thinking of something; then he put his blackthorn stick on top of the tomb, stood a while longer, and on going from the graveyard left the stick behind him. He went home and ate his supper. After supper John went to a neighbour's house where young people used to meet of an evening, and the three girls happened to be there that time. John was very quiet, so that every one noticed him.

"What is troubling you this evening, John?" asked one of the girls.

"Oh, I am sorry for my beautiful blackthorn," said he.

"Did you lose it?"

"I did not," said John; "but I left it on the top of the tomb next to the grave of the man who was buried to-day, and whichever of you three will go for it is the woman I'll marry. Well, Mary, will you go for my stick?" asked he.

"Faith, then, I will not," said Mary.

"Well, Peggy, will you go?"

"If I were without a man for ever," said Peggy, "I wouldn't go."

"Well, Kate," said he to the third, "will you go for my stick? If you go I'll marry you."

"Stand to your word," said Kate, "and I'll bring the stick."

"Believe me, that I will," said John.

Kate left the company behind her, and went for the stick. The graveyard was three miles away and the walk was a long one. Kate came to the place at last and made out the tomb by the fresh grave. When she had her hand on the blackthorn a voice called from the tomb:

"Leave the stick where it is and open this tomb for me."

Kate began to tremble and was greatly in dread, but something was forcing her to open the tomb—she couldn't help herself.

"Take the lid off now," said the dead man when Kate had the door open and was inside in the tomb, "and take me out of this—take me on your back."

Afraid to refuse, she took the lid from the coffin, raised the dead man on her back, and walked on in the way he directed. She walked about the distance of a mile. The load, being very heavy, was near breaking her back and killing her. She walked half a mile farther and came to a village; the houses were at the side of the road.

"Take me to the first house," said the dead man.

She took him.

"Oh, we cannot go in here," said he, when they came near. "The people have clean water inside, and they have holy water, too. Take me to the next house."

She went to the next house.

"We cannot go in there," said he, when she stopped in front of the door. "They have clean water, and there is holy water as well."

She went to the third house.

"Go in here," said the dead man. "There is neither clean water nor holy water in this place; we can stop in it."

They went in.

"Bring a chair now and put me sitting at the side of the fire. Then find me something to eat and to drink."

She placed him in a chair by the hearth, searched the house, found a dish of oatmeal and brought it. "I have nothing to give you to drink but dirty water," said she.

"Bring me a dish and a razor."

She brought the dish and the razor.

"Come, now," said he, "to the room above."

They went up to the room, where three young men, sons of the man of the house, were sleeping in bed, and Kate had to hold the dish while the dead man was drawing their blood.

"Let the father and mother have that," said he, "in return for the dirty water"; meaning that if there was clean water in the house he wouldn't have taken the blood of the young men. He closed their wounds in the way that there was no sign of a cut on them. "Mix this now with the meal, get a dish of it for yourself and another for me."

She got two plates and put the oatmeal in it after mixing it, and brought two spoons. Kate wore a handkerchief on her head; she put this under her neck and tied it; she was pretending to eat, but she was putting the food to hide in the handkerchief till her plate was empty.

"Have you your share eaten?" asked the dead man.

"I have," answered Kate.

"I'll have mine finished this minute," said he, and soon after he gave her the empty dish. She put the dishes back in the dresser, and didn't mind washing them. "Come, now," said he, "and take me back to the place where you found me."

"Oh, how can I take you back; you are too great a load; 'twas killing me you were when I brought you." She was in dread of going from the house again.

"You are stronger after that food than what you were in coming; take me back to my grave."

She went against her will. She rolled up the food inside the handkerchief. There was a deep hole in the wall of the kitchen by the door, where the bar was slipped in when they barred the door; into this hole she put the handkerchief. In going back she shortened the road by going through a big field at command of the dead man. When they were at the top of the field she asked, was there any cure for those young men whose blood was drawn?

"There is no cure," said he, "except one. If any of that food had been spared, three bits of it in each young man's mouth would bring them to life again, and they'd never know of their death."

"Then," said Kate in her own mind, "that cure is to be had."

"Do you see this field?" asked the dead man.

"I do."

"Well, there is as much gold buried in it as would make rich people of all who belong to you. Do you see the three leachtans [piles of small stones]? Underneath each of them is a pot of gold."

The dead man looked around for a while; then Kate went on, without stopping, till she came to the wall of the graveyard, and just then they heard the cock crow.

"The cock is crowing," said Kate; "it's time for me to be going home."

"It is not time yet," said the dead man; "that is a bastard cock."

A moment after that another cock crowed. "There the cocks are crowing a second time," said she. "No," said the dead man, "that is a bastard cock again; that's no right bird." They came to the mouth of the tomb and a cock crowed the third time.

"Well," said the girl, "that must be the right cock."

"Ah, my girl, that cock has saved your life for you. But for him I would have you with me in the grave for evermore, and if I knew this cock would crow before I was in the grave you wouldn't have the knowledge you have now of the field and the gold. Put me into the coffin where you found me. Take your time and settle me well. I cannot meddle with you now, and 'tis sorry I am to part with you."

"Will you tell me who you are?" asked Kate.

"Have you ever heard your father or mother mention a man called Edward Derrihy or his son Michael?"

"It's often I heard tell of them," replied the girl.

"Well, Edward Derrihy was my father; I am Michael. That blackthorn that you came for to-night to this graveyard was the lucky stick for you, but if you had any thought of the danger that was before you, you wouldn't be here. Settle me carefully and close the tomb well behind you."

She placed him in the coffin carefully, closed the door behind her, took the blackthorn stick, and away home with Kate. The night was far spent when she came. She was tired, and it's good reason the girl had. She thrust the stick into the thatch above the door of the house and rapped. Her sister rose up and opened the door.

"Where did you spend the night?" asked the sister. "Mother will kill you in the morning for spending the whole night from home."

"Go to bed," answered Kate, "and never mind me."

They went to bed, and Kate fell asleep the minute she touched the bed, she was that tired after the night.

When the father and mother of the three young men rose next morning, and there was no sign of their sons, the mother went to the room to call them, and there she found the three dead. She began to screech and wring her hands. She ran to the road screaming and wailing. All the neighbours crowded around to know what trouble was on her. She told them her three sons were lying dead in their bed after the night. Very soon the report spread in every direction. When Kate's father and mother heard it they hurried off to the house of the dead men. When they came home Kate was still in bed; the mother took a stick and began to beat the girl for being out all the night and in bed all the day.

"Get up now, you lazy stump of a girl," said she, "and go to the wake house; your neighbour's three sons are dead."

Kate took no notice of this. "I am very tired and sick," said she. "You'd better spare me and give me a drink."

The mother gave her a drink of milk and a bite to eat, and in the middle of the day she rose up.

"'Tis a shame for you not to be at the wake house yet," said the mother; "hurry over now."

When Kate reached the house there was a great crowd of people before her and great wailing. She did not cry, but was looking on. The father was as if wild, going up and down the house wringing his hands.

"Be quiet," said Kate. "Control yourself."

"How can I do that, my dear girl, and my three fine sons lying dead in the house?"

"What would you give," asked Kate, "to the person who would bring life to them again?"

"Don't be vexing me," said the father.

"It's neither vexing you I am nor trifling," said Kate. "I can put the life in them again."

"If it was true that you could do that, I would give you all that I have inside the house and outside as well."

"All I want from you," said Kate, "is the eldest son to marry and Gort na Leachtan [the field of the stone heaps] as fortune."

"My dear, you will have that from me with the greatest blessing."

"Give me the field in writing from yourself, whether the son will marry me or not."

He gave her the field in his handwriting. She told all who were inside in the wake-house to go outside the door, every man and woman of them. Some were laughing at her and more were crying, thinking it was mad she was. She bolted the door inside, and went to the place where she left the handkerchief, found it, and put three bites of the oatmeal and the blood in the mouth of each young man, and as soon as she did that the three got their natural colour, and they looked like men sleeping. She opened the door, then called on all to come inside, and told the father to go and wake his sons.

He called each one by name, and as they woke they seemed very tired after their night's rest; they put on their clothes, and were greatly surprised to see all the people around. "How is this?" asked the eldest brother.

"Don't you know of anything that came over you in the night?" asked the father.

"We do not," said the sons. "We remember nothing at all since we fell asleep last evening."

The father then told them everything, but they could not believe it. Kate went away home and told her father and mother of her night's journey to and from the graveyard, and said that she would soon tell them more.

That day she met John.

"Did you bring the stick?" asked he.

"Find your own stick," said she, "and never speak to me again in your life."

In a week's time she went to the house of the three young men, and said to the father, "I have come for what you promised me."

"You'll get that with my blessing," said the father. He called the eldest son aside then and asked would he marry Kate, their neighbour's daughter. "I will," said the son. Three days after that the two were married and had a fine wedding. For three weeks they enjoyed a pleasant life without toil or trouble; then Kate said, "This will not do for us; we must be working. Come with me to-morrow and I'll give yourself and brothers plenty to do, and my own father and brothers as well."

She took them next day to one of the stone heaps in Gort na Leachtan. "Throw these stones to one side," said she.

They thought that she was losing her senses, but she told them that they'd soon see for themselves what she was doing. They went to work and kept at it till they had six feet deep of a hole dug; then they met with a flat stone three feet square and an iron hook in the middle of it.

"Sure there must be something underneath this," said the men. They lifted the flag, and under it was a pot of gold. All were very happy then. "There is more gold yet in the place," said Kate. "Come, now, to the other heap." They removed that heap, dug down, and found another pot of gold. They removed the third pile and found a third pot full of gold. On the side of the third pot was an inscription, and they could not make out what it was. After emptying it they placed the pot by the side of the door.

About a month later a poor scholar walked the way, and as he was going in at the door he saw the old pot and the letters on the side of it. He began to study the letters.

"You must be a good scholar if you can read what's on that pot," said the young man.

"I can," said the poor scholar, "and here it is for you. 'There is a deal more at the south side of each pot.'"

The young man said nothing, but putting his hand in his pocket, gave the poor scholar a good day's hire. When he was gone they went to work and found a deal more of gold at the south side of each stone heap. They were very happy then and very rich, and bought several farms and built fine houses, and it was supposed by all of them in the latter end that it was Derrihy's money that was buried under the leachtans, but they could give no correct account of that, and sure why need they care? When they died they left property to make their children rich to the seventh generation.

Murderous Ghosts

THE following things happened about sixty years ago. In those times people used to go nine and ten miles to mass, especially of a Christmas Day. Four men in the parish of Drummond went to Cahirdonnell to mass on Christmas and didn't start for home till after nightfall. The four were a young master with his servant-boy, and two married men, small farmers. When they came to a certain side path the young master with his servant-boy turned in there to go home, and the two others followed the main road. The men on the road were not far away when they heard a wild screech in the field.

"What can that be?" asked one. "Something must be happening; the night is dark."

They heard a second screech, but went on without stopping.

Next morning a messenger came to inquire where did they leave the young master and the servant-boy, and the men said, "We left them when they turned from the main road to go home through the field."

"They didn't come," said the messenger, "and I'm in dread they are killed."

All the neighbours went to search for the two, and found the

young man dead, a long distance out from the path, and he black
and blue, as people are always when killed by ghosts or fairies.
They couldn't find the servant-boy high or low.

The father of the young man sat up waiting all the night
before for his son. About midnight he heard a terrible wind
blowing around the house outside. He rose, bolted the door,
and sat down by the fire again. A few minutes later there was
a great struggle in front of the house and a noise as of some
one making a kick at the door to open it. This was the servant-
boy, who came to the house before the ghost and tried to
break in. When he couldn't move the door he ran to the hag-
gart, where there were two stacks of hay. He sprang to one of
the stacks to climb up and defend himself from the top of the
stack. The ghost pulled him down, but he brought his two fists
full of dry hay with him. The ghost drove him out of the hag-
gart and hunted him through seven fields to a river. Next day
he was found on the bank dead, and he all black and blue. His
suspenders broke, and he would never have been killed but
that they broke: the cross on his back made by the suspenders would have saved him. His two fists were still grasping
the hay.

About ten years later this very same ghost, a woman, attacked
a man who was out late and was coming home with a hatchet on
his shoulder and a saw in his hand. The man used the saw well,
striking her with it, and she couldn't get at him through the
steel. She knocked three or four falls out of him, but he rose
each time; she struck one of his eyes and he lost the use of it. At
last, after a great struggle, he came to a place where a stream of
water was running across the road, and she couldn't follow him
through that, for no ghost can follow a person through water.
When he reached the other side he stood and looked at her.
"You have yourself saved; you are a strong man: the best that
came before me since I killed such and such a man ten years
ago," said she, mentioning the servant-boy and the master, "but
if I haven't the better of you yet, you have a keepsake from me
that will stay with you."

The man went home, took to the bed, and didn't live six
months. He was pining away every day till he died.

Some time later a man was drowned in Waterville, and he was one of the two farmers who came on Christmas night from mass at Cahirdonnell with the master and servant-boy that were killed. Three months after this man's death his wife went with her brother matchmaking in the town. The brother settled a match between herself and a man living in Drummond parish, which is over the mountains from Cahircivcen. She got marriage quittance from the priest in Cahirciveen, paid ten shillings for it, and put it in her pocket.

That evening she and the brother started to go to the house of a friend who lived next door to the man she was going to marry, for it's there the wedding was to be. She kept the marriage quittance in her pocket. When they were about half-way it commenced to snow, and when they were half a mile from the house she began to fall every minute.

"Yerra, what is the matter?" asked the brother.

"My first husband is killing me!" said she.

The brother tried his best to save her, but no use; he got blows enough himself and saw nobody. At last he took off his coat. He had a stick in his hand; he stuck the stick down in the ground and hung the coat on it to mark the place, for the land all around was white from snow. He left his sister there and ran to the friend's house (the house was no more than a quarter of a mile away) to bring help and save the sister. When the two came with a few neighbours the woman was dead, and the place for ten perches around was torn up as with a horse and plough.

All the people said, and the priest himself agreed with them, that it was against the rules for the woman to carry the marriage quittance, and if the brother had carried it the ghost would have spared them both.

I knew a man named Tom Moran who lived a few miles from Cahirciveen. I knew Tom and his wife very well, but at the time my story begins Tom wasn't married.

One time he was kept late in town by the shoemaker, and on the road home he met a strange priest on horseback. The priest stopped him. "Why are you out so late, my good man?" asked the priest; "'tis in your bed you should be. The night outside belongs to the dead and the house to the living."

"Why are you outside yourself?" asked Tom.

"'Tis my business to be out at all times," said the priest. "Is it often you are out at night?"

"It is then," said Tom.

"Go home, now," said the priest, "the night is no time for travelling."

When Tom came home he put his white horse outside in a little field so as to be able to put his hands on him easily and have no delay in the morning, for he was to go to the strand very early for seaweed. He wasn't long in bed when he heard the horse galloping around the house and making a great noise. Tom ran out in his shirt to see what the trouble was, but if he did he couldn't come near the horse.

Out on to the road with the horse and Tom after him, in shirt and bare feet. Tom followed till he came to a very lonesome place at the side of a graveyard, about two miles from his own house. The horse turned in there, and Tom followed closely till they came to a field, where the horse disappeared; and no wonder, for the field was full up of men and horses. Tom stepped aside into a corner. All the crowd moved from the field and went past him towards the road. When they went out the road was covered with people and horses moving towards Cahirciveen. All at once they shot away quickly and Tom came home alone. He found his horse in the field where he put him at first. It was a fairy horse that gave him the turn to the graveyard.

Some time after this Tom Moran married in this parish and his wife died in twelve months after the marriage. Nine or ten months after her death Tom was going home one night from Cahirciveen. He was matchmaking all day to know could he find a new wife, and he wasn't above a quarter of a mile from the town when he met the dead woman.

"You are here, you ruffian," said she. "Isn't it soon for you to be marrying again? You didn't give time to my footprints to leave the puddle in the yard or the hair to fall from my head in the grave before you are looking for a second wife, but I'll pay you well to-night for your conduct."

She went at him then and knocked him, but he rose up and walked on. She made after him and took another fall out of him.

"Now," said she, "if I don't take a third fall out of you before you go to Needham's gate you will be saved; but if I do you are done for."

Just at the gate she knocked him a third time and left him. Tom made his way home and sent for the priest and told him everything, he told the neighbours as well. He didn't live more than three or four days. [Needham's gate is about half a mile from Cahirciveen.]

NOTE.—The tales from "John Cokeley and the Fairy" to the end were told by Dyeermud Sheehy, a cartman for years between Killarney and Cahirciveen.